A REWILDER'S GUIDE

to Outdoor Adventure

Self-healing in Nature

PATRICK JOSEPH CLARK

Paperback ISBN: 978-1-953031-06-8
Ebook ISBN: 978-1-953031-07-5

Library of Congress Control Number 2025908251

Edited by Roberta Binder, Heidi Hansen, Chris Knight
Book design by Tamara Cribley
Cover design by Heidi Hansen

Printed in the United States of America

Published by Scynthefy Press, LLC
https://www.scynthefy.com/

Contact us at

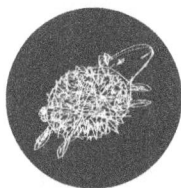

www.lucky-sheep.com

Dedicated to all the people who believed in me and helped make this book possible—especially Roberta Binder, Heidi Marie Hanson, Aisha Johnson Adams, Mary Giles, Linsi Deyo, Krishna Kant Shunkla, Rebecca Mimms, John Clark, and all the Lucky Sheep customers who took the first step before this became a trend.

Also dedicated to all seekers of Truth, Knowledge, Wisdom, Beauty and Peace—may the peace of nature penetrate our hearts as we each walk our own hero's journey.

Table of Contents

Introduction

How I Discovered Forest Bathing and Natural Fibers

Years ago, I was hiking barefoot up a mountain trail with a friend, sharing my crazy idea to reinvent backpacking gear to align with the philosophy of barefoot walking. There was something different about this hike than most of my previous hikes. I was not wearing shoes, and I was seeing how far I could take it. I was breaking a fundamental rule from my Outdoor Leadership training to always wear sturdy boots to protect my feet. But walking barefoot was reawakening my connection to Earth. This was during the beginning of the Rewilding movement, and people were waking up to the need to connect to Earth in a new way. I was grounding myself, realigning my circadian rhythms, expanding my resilience to cold mountain streams, and, most importantly, healing from twenty years of multiple chemical sensitivities. I began wondering—how many other outdoor practices could I adapt to this philosophy?

The Birth of a New Outdoor Philosophy

What first led me down this path was my struggle with autoimmune dysfunction and multiple chemical sensitivities. I discovered I was allergic to modern backpacking gear—tents, sleeping bags, and synthetic materials loaded with chemicals. In my mind, I envisioned an entire camping setup made from organic fabrics. There was just one problem: I didn't know how to sew.

Over the next decade, I learned. I experimented with natural fiber fabrics, tested different designs, and, eventually, I invented a full line of natural outdoor gear—what is now the Lucky Sheep™ brand.

But my journey wasn't just about creating gear. It was about rediscovering a way of being in nature.

Healing Through Nature

In those early days, my sensitivities were so extreme that even the natural mold in the forest triggered reactions. But after years of following a Primal/Paleo diet and eliminating toxins from my home, my body grew stronger. Eventually, I could sleep outside again without reacting.

That's when I began my experiments—crafting an organic canvas tent coated with beeswax and a wool sleeping bag. Equipped with a few days' worth of fresh Paleo food, I set off into the Smoky Mountains and Pisgah National Forest, searching for healing sanctuaries by water.

The routine was simple but profound:

- Sleep deeply in the fresh mountain air.

- Wake up and bathe in the cold creek.

- Sunbathe on warm rocks.

- Hike, eat, rest, swim, and repeat.

It felt like I had discovered the fountain of youth—a synergy between Earth, sun, and nature that was bringing me back to life.

When I returned from these trips, I would tell my friends, sounding like a madman. But some were intrigued and eager to learn my methods.

The Spiritual Awakening of Forest Bathing

My journey wasn't just physical—it was also deeply spiritual and emotional. As I immersed myself in the wilderness, I realized that forest bathing had long been a part of ancient yogic practices. Seekers throughout history have retreated into nature to break through mental barriers and access higher states of consciousness.

For me, being near a moving creek or waterfall became a portal to something beyond my everyday awareness. The smells, the rushing water on my skin, the sun dissolving my stress—all of it combined into an alchemy of healing. My meditation deepened, my mind expanded, and I experienced moments of pure, causeless joy and bliss. There was something so different than my previous hiking and camping experiences, which were more of a mental approach and using the herd mentality of the outdoor community with set belief systems. Here, I was truly breaking free to be myself and follow my intuition. I could hear an inner voice that wasn't audible in the hustle and bustle of everyday life.

An Early Experience with Failure of Modern Gear

Years before the just-mentioned experience, I went on a winter backpacking trip in the Great Smoky Mountains National Park, hiking the leafless, tree-covered trail up to Mount LeConte. Little did I know what I was getting into and where it would lead. A buddy came with me the first day and night; we crossed a few ice-cold creeks barefoot, taking off boots and rolling up pants legs. My friend then turned back as planned. I was to continue a couple more nights on my own following the Appalachian Trail.

At some point, near the top of the mountain where the trail intersected the Appalachian Trail, I lost the trail. I walked for a time under the bare branches and silent gray sky, not knowing exactly where I was. Even though I had spent nights camping and backpacking and was proficient in topographic map navigation, I was a little worried since I was simply "dead reckoning" my way to the top of the mountain in a very remote wilderness. I managed to make it to the Appalachian Trail right before dark. I made an emergency camp and, after a simple meal, fell asleep.

I woke up the next day and discovered that I was sweating in my sleeping bag. To my surprise, the landscape had transformed overnight. Everything was covered in snow, and apparently, the tent had piled with snow that had then sagged down to my body level. I was overheating because the snow added insulation similar to an igloo, and the synthetic clothing and sleeping bag would not allow proper ventilation of my body heat.

I packed up and hiked along the trail to the first trail shelter, where I hung up my gear so it could dry in the cold wind and sun. I had gotten wet from overheating in my synthetic gear, then cold from being wet in the cold and wind. Then, I packed up again to continue. Unfortunately, however, after I had hiked for a full day through the snow and cold winds, damp and sweaty, as well as having walked through icy creeks the day before, I just didn't feel I could go on. I felt depleted and chilled. I had maxed out, gone to my edge and spent my reserves. I decided to hitchhike to the nearest town, Bryson City, and call my buddy to come pick me up.

There had to be a better way. Someday, I would discover not only how to build my body up to match the elements and eat food that would generate body heat but also how to use techniques and gear that would work with the changing conditions of outdoor adventure. All these discoveries ended up revolutionizing my approach to the outdoors and my relationship with the elements.

I have long been an outdoor gear nut, trying every latest technical invention and following the dominant paradigm about what kind of gear works best. I majored in Outdoor Recreation in college and I took a Wilderness Education Association Outdoor Leadership Training with Dr. Paul Petzoldt. Petzoldt is the founder of NOLS, Outward Bound, and Wilderness Education Association and is known as "the Grandfather of Outdoor Leadership." During the 1990s, I published a zine called *Kokopelli Notes: Walking and Biking for a Greener Planet,* which aimed to encourage people to integrate the outdoor lifestyle into their everyday lives. This experience gave me a taste of a lot of the latest gear and inventions both in the biking and hiking worlds.

Later, I developed a debilitating illness called Multiple Chemical Sensitivities, which made me allergic to many things I had previously taken for granted. Harmful chemicals are ubiquitous in our modern world and challenging to escape. I spent the next decade learning how to eliminate plastic in my house, go organic with my clothing, bedding, furniture, household cleaners, and personal hygiene items, and detox my body.

I was also learning about barefoot walking, earthing, Raw Paleo Diet/Primal Diet, sun gazing, cold plunging, and things that later became known collectively as "Rewilding." These practices opened up a whole new world for me, and my health started coming back; I was thawing out from a decade of decline.

The funny thing is my outdoor gear—which was supposed to get me closer to nature—was still the most toxic, unnatural thing left in my belongings.

Determined to find a solution, I embarked on a quest for the perfect backpacking adventure. Frustratingly, I would always come home from a few days in the woods feeling exhausted and depleted. Something wasn't right. Going into nature, with all the health benefits it can offer, just wasn't proving itself to be the health spa experience I knew it could be. How could I increase my vitality and have gains in homeostasis and fitness as a result of going into nature rather than experiencing depletion and losses in homeostasis and fitness? How could I come home feeling like I had had a nice workout but without needing days to recover?

Upon discovering the Paleo Diet, I experienced a new relationship with the elements. Now, when exposing myself to the forces of nature, such as the ground, sun, cold water, and physical exertion, I started to feel good. Before this, I had always been cold and not nearly as rugged as I wanted to be to withstand the rigors of the outdoors. But with the new diet, I experienced new gains in lean body mass, strength, and endurance, as well as the ability to sleep well and feel grounded and at ease even in stressful situations.

During this process, I also discovered a major difference between synthetic versus natural fiber clothing and bedding. People were rediscovering the power of wool to outperform its synthetic counterparts keeping metabolism and sleep at their optimal levels and keeping the body dry in harsh outdoor environments. I noticed that I slept so much better with wool and, in fact, had never actually felt truly warm in down and synthetic. I experimented with living in a tipi year-round, using only natural fibers, which was my attempt to test out the entire Paleo lifestyle and see what it would do. I ended up becoming even stronger and more robust, as well as developing a new relationship with the outdoors. I felt I could go anywhere at any time of year and feel far more comfortable than when I was following the herd mentality of consuming grain-based food and using synthetic gear, acting in accordance with other people's opinions.

I pieced together a set of backpacking gear from scraps of fabric and wool clothing found at thrift stores, tested it for several years, and realized at one point that I had invented a new backpacking style. This approach is based on replicating our ancestral heritage as much as possible. It allows us to enter nature with a new set of gear, techniques, and consciousness. This book will explain my process of discovery as well as break down my backpacking system into an organized set of principles that you can easily adapt to your life.

PART I

Rewilding

Rewilding and the Ancestral Health Movement: Improve Your Health and Longevity in Nature

What is Rewilding?

Rewilding is a paradigm and lifestyle that brings us closer to nature and to our primal state of being, leading to increased health and vitality, among many other benefits. The definition of primal: connected with the earliest origins of life; relating to an early stage in evolutionary development; primeval; first; original; of first importance; first in time; primitive; fundamental; basic. By "our primal state of being," I mean the parts of ourselves that are ancient and fundamental to our nature. When in our primal state of being, we may experience feelings that our ancient ancestors may have felt of belonging with the animals, trees, land, cycles, seasons, weather, and feeling at one with and being an inherent part of all the elements of the natural world.

There is nothing parallel to spending time in wild places to reconnect with the soul and experience the tantalizing sensations of nature. Hiking, camping, and backpacking enable us to experience this reconnection with nature by giving us the opportunity to spend extended periods outdoors. To me this is the ultimate goal of Rewilding, and beyond that, the ultimate goal of life.

Western civilization has taken Manifest Destiny too far. The Western mindset has conquered nature from sea to shining sea and is left with a spiritual and cultural desert. The Rewilding movement gives us a pathway to reclaim our birthright and to feel human again. Because without nature, we are nothing.

One of my early forest bathing base camps.

The Health Benefits of Spending Time in Nature

Rewilding counteracts nature-deficit disorder and over-domestication, modern-day conditions that come from being almost totally disconnected from nature and lead to illnesses of mind, emotions, spirit, and body.

> "According to the Environmental Protection Agency (EPA), the average American spends 93% of their life indoors. 87% of their life indoors, then another 6% of their life in automobiles. That's only 7% of your entire life outdoors. That's only one half of one day per week outdoors."
>
> ~ Frontiers in Psychology

"… the average American spends…
only one half of one day per week outdoors."

My early days of forest bathing

Contact with nature has been tied to better health in a plenitude of studies. Time spent in and around tree-lined streets, gardens, parks, and forested and agricultural lands is consistently linked to objective, long-term positive health outcomes. More neighborhood greenness has been consistently tied to better life expectancy and all-cause mortality. Science strongly indicates that we are dependent on consistent contact with nature for our well-being and longevity.

The range of adverse health outcomes tied to being cut off from nature is startling; it includes depression and anxiety disorder, diabetes mellitus, attention-deficit/hyperactivity disorder (ADHD), various infectious diseases, cancer, more difficulty healing from surgery, obesity, birth outcomes, cardiovascular disease, musculoskeletal complaints, migraines, respiratory disease, and others, reviewed below. The less green in a person's surroundings, the higher their risk of morbidity and mortality, even when controlling for socioeconomic status and other possible confounding variables.

The bottom line is the modern Western lifestyle is making us sick. The things we take for granted, like shoes, living indoors, sitting, using artificial lighting, and eating over-processed foods, are creating "neolithic" diseases, a.k.a. Modern Diseases. That means diseases not found before modern times; diseases of domestication, which means most diseases.

What is the Ancestral Health Movement?

The Ancestral Health movement researches the lifestyles and environments of ancient humans, analyzes their overall benefits to health and well-being, and endeavors to put them into practice today. Rewilding is pretty much the same philosophy as Ancestral Health—the philosophy of finding and experiencing the many benefits of living close to nature and incorporating natural ways of living into daily life.

The Ancestral Health movement has determined that ancient humans were much healthier than we are today, possessing incredible bone density, physical abilities, and longevity. And they didn't need a complex medical system to stay that way; they were self-sustaining within their environment.

Ways Ancient Humans Maintained Peak Levels of Health

- **Diet.** Eating a nutrient-dense native diet high in fats, and meats which were balanced in minerals and vitamins.

- **Grounding.** Being grounded on the earth by living close to the ground and walking with minimal or no shoes in the sun.

- **Light Cycle Attunement and Alignment.** Being exposed to natural daylight cycles which synchronize circadian rhythms, which increases sleep quality and cellular energy.

- **EMF-Free Life.** Never being exposed to power lines and cell towers such as non-native electromagnetic fields (EMFs) and radio frequencies (RFs).

- **Chemical-Free Life.** Not being exposed to toxic, endocrine-disrupting chemicals that accumulate in the body, increase body burden, and lead to toxic overload.

- **Constant Low-Impact Movement.** Engaging in consistent natural low-impact movement (instead of sitting long hours every day). This keeps the metabolism at a good rate.

- **Temperature Exposure and Adaptation.** Being exposed to the natural seasonal temperatures of where they lived instead of in artificially heated or cooled environments.

- **Real Living Water.** Drinking pure, wild, structured water. This detoxifies and hydrates the cells, which unstructured and polluted tap water cannot do.

- **Tree Aromas and Forest Therapy.** Being exposed to terpenes and phytoncides, aerosols produced by trees that helped protect them from parasites and disease. These compounds are beneficial to human health. Breathing these and other elements of forest air is a component of forest therapy.

- **Negative Ions.** Being frequently exposed to negative ions, the universal energy donor that occurs in mist, dew, fog, and near moving water such as creeks and waterfalls.

Toxicity and Deficiency

Most people are not aware of the Ancestral Health discoveries that run counter to most mainstream ideas. There wasn't any reason to question anything until so many of us were getting sick and then got fed up with the lack of answers from medical authorities. A few decades of diverse research from around the globe have come to one conclusion: most modern sickness is a result of our modern-day environment, diet, and lifestyle. This can be summed up in two words: toxicity and deficiency. Terms like "sick building syndrome," "metabolic disorder," and "diseases of civilization" reflect this dismal state of affairs.

My journey was no exception. I spent twenty years on a downward spiral of ill health until I discovered the Paleo Diet, Rewilding, and Ancestral Health approaches, which brought me back to life and gave me a second chance.

When we Rewild ourselves, we reverse engineer certain parts of Western Culture that have laid waste to the environment and disconnected us from nature and our bodies. Through education and effort, we slowly turn the ship of our life around from modern disease to ancient health.

The Tipi Experiment

I started experimenting with different ways of sleeping, as I noticed I had interesting results depending on things like the environment and materials I used. I especially noticed amazing things happening when sleeping near water and later found it is known to be conducive to astral travel. The world started becoming more fun, intriguing and multi-dimensional as my various explorations unfolded.

I moved into a tipi to test these ideas in real life.

How did this even start? As a kid, I noticed the magic of certain places. Or in other words, I was drawn to go to the edge. Instead of sitting in my room to read a book, I would climb a tree and sit on a limb. I was always on the lookout for the most exciting and interesting places possible. Most kids are the same, and cats as well. The difference is, I took it to the extremes.

Consider this, a grown adult moving out of a house and into a tipi, even in the middle of winter. Why would I do this? Because I was following my bliss. Because there was magic happening everywhere and at that time, I felt the houses were cutting me off from it. Some of my friends thought I had taken my lifestyle too far, and were warning me of the dangers of sleeping in the cold! Yet, I was on a quest, no one could tell where it would go, not even I. I was following the energy. I was at one with the process of life and this is what wanted to happen next.

I was tasting the feeling of sleeping with wool and on the ground, during all seasons. I was testing all the theories of grounding, circadian balancing, cold therapy, metabolism boosting, thyroid enhancing food. My process was that of a minimalist, to take away that which was in the way. Unlike other approaches of buying gadgets to try to get the ancestral health effects. I was living in a primordial health spa. And I cracked the code of how to be at ease in the cold, and unafraid of all the bumps in the night that keep others from this paradise.

Why Camping / Backpacking?

These practices are the only things that get us in touch with nature for enough time and depth to have a feeling for living on the land. Backpacking is a convenient way to experience raw nature without exiting our modern lifestyle which wouldn't be practical. Day hiking is great. Gardening and playing outside is great. But spending the night and extended time in places where the human footprint isn't noticeable or barely noticeable is essential to remind us of who we are and where we came from. Without this, we become over-domesticated and have no baseline. Nature is our source and it gives us much information on many levels. We need to know our source and use that to imprint our body and soul without human interference. We need our human mother and our earth mother to really know where we came from. Without experiencing nature deeply, we are like orphans on an alien planet.

And being in nature brings us to the healing properties we have been denied in our over-industrialized world. We can access the realms of our inner nature, slow down, and access the silence within. The issues we are dealing with in our personal lives come out in front of us; we go deeper, and we see the nature of the mind and consciousness as we access more silence and more depth. All of this is because we have a break from the Western world, which has shaped our belief system and dictated values that are not in our best interests.

Sometimes, we don't realize the impact of the messages surrounding us. We are inundated by messages that are coming from a place of fear and survival. Also, the media is bombarding us with images and messages that tell us that we aren't perfect and that we need all kinds of improvements to make our lives better. When we can disengage for a little while, a new set of feelings and impressions comes in from the Universe, Nature, Divine, God, or whatever you want to call the realm beyond the mind and self. If we can let these imprint our consciousness, we will come back renewed and more in alignment with purpose…more in touch with our inner truth and not following the chaotic influences of the outer world.

I have researched and experimented extensively and developed a camping and backpacking system that is relatively light, weighing slightly more than modern lightweight backpacking gear, and yet helps us to feel alive, recharge ourselves, and interact with the elements the way we are designed to. By using nature as a primal health spa, we can not only regenerate ourselves and merge with nature better but also increase performance without draining our battery—losing electrons, minerals, and cellular energy. Hiking and camping offer a perfect opportunity for a primordial experience. This book provides a practical guide about how to rewild your backpacking expeditions, but it also goes deeper than that into ways you can rewild yourself, including mind, body, and spirit. I hope you will enjoy my journey of discovery as you find your way into this approach to life.

Epigenetics and Ancestral Health: Harnessing Circadian Rhythms and Mitochondrial Health for Optimal Well-Being

In the quest for improved health and longevity, researchers and health enthusiasts have begun to explore the fascinating realm of epigenetics, shedding light on how our genes interact with our environment to influence our overall well-being. One profound aspect of this emerging field is the connection between ancestral health practices and the optimization of two crucial elements: circadian rhythms and mitochondrial health.

Our ancestors, who lived closer to nature, aligned their daily lives with the natural world, and this alignment played a pivotal role in their robust health. Today, we are rediscovering the benefits of these ancient practices and incorporating them into our modern lifestyles to achieve better health outcomes. In this brief overview, we will delve into the profound effects of balancing circadian rhythms and preserving mitochondrial health through practices such as exposure to natural light, adherence to ancestral diets, the influence of magnetism, temperature regulation, and the importance of movement.

By understanding and implementing these principles, we can unlock the potential to optimize our epigenetic expression, reducing the risk of chronic diseases and promoting vitality in our lives. Let's explore how these ancient practices can provide a blueprint for modern-day health and well-being.

In a nutshell, this new approach to health explores how our environment influences our biology. From that, we glean the essentials to vibrant, robust health, supercharged immunity, healing from disease and injury, and basically the fountain of youth.

Advantages of Ancestral Health

- Yoke your body to optimal circadian rhythms.

- Supercharge your mitochondria.

- Balance your hormones naturally.

- Feel at ease in the cold and heat.

- Improve alignment, flexibility, and mobility.

- Improve sleep quality, so you wake up refreshed and ready to hit the trail.

- Be comfortable when hiking and camping using natural fiber clothing.

- Feel energized by sun exposure without burning.

How the Environment and Lifestyle Effects Our Health

Food is only one of the things we eat. The study of Epigenetics and Ancestral Health reveals that our bodies also absorb other elements and phenomena from our environment, which in turn influence our health. By looking at the way our ancestors lived, we can discover vital factors determining how we can optimize our metabolism and be able to withstand the rigors of outdoor living.

Elements and Lifestyle Choices

- **Light.** The natural cycles of night/day, which in turn regulate hormone function and circadian rhythms

- **Magnetism.** The influence of gravity from the earth. We are not receiving the full benefit of this when surrounded by power lines and radio frequencies. The remedy for this is Earthing and Grounding with Earth's electromagnetic field and Schumann's Frequency.

- **Movement.** Consistent, low-impact exercise keeps our metabolism fired up, which prevents us from metabolic syndrome, loss of energy, and weight gain, which is the disease of a sedentary life.

- **Temperature.** Exposure to the outside temperature extremes of hot and cold tells our body how to synchronize the many biological processes that also join the light cycles and diet.

- **Diet.** Food grown in a latitude close to the one we live in will keep us well adapted to the light cycles and temperatures of that same region. This means that closer to the poles and colder climates would require more animal proteins and fats. The equatorial and warmer climates would require more carbohydrates.

- **Water.** Water that is structured will help the cellular communication in our bodies to fire efficiently which is key to metabolic health. Structured water is wild water found in nature. Tap water is destructured.

Doing all of the right things and eliminating the wrong things is a recipe for Ancestral Health. We can then harness the regenerative powers of nature to supercharge metabolism, turn back the biological clock, optimize weight and body composition, establish consistent deep sleep, and power our mitochondria. But most importantly, to simply feel good again.

CHAPTER 2

The Health-Enhancing Practice of Grounding

Things like power lines, the wiring inside houses, cell phones, and cell towers are creating what is called nnEMFs, or non-native Electromagnetic Fields. I have been sensitive to nnEMFs for some time, and I have had an intuitive knack for avoiding harmful things even before I knew they were harmful. For instance, I started sleeping outside in my yard when I was a teenager because I felt better. This relates to the concepts of grounding or earthing.

I've had the good fortune to be friends with two women who are EHS or Electromagnetic Hypersensitive. I have learned so much about electromagnetic fields and how they affect us in ways that we don't normally know from these women, who can each perceive the most minute change in the energy field around them. They would call to my attention to things I could not perceive, such as proximity to a dangerous power line or cell tower. I learned about EMF Hygiene, such as how to keep my cell phone on airplane mode or turn it off when not using it.

All of this is understood by science and is measurable with EMF Meters. The question becomes, why do we need earthing in the first place? The reason is that we are exposed to harmful non-native EMFs that unyoke, or unground, us from our native field. Earthing is a way to recalibrate our body to the actual native EMF field, which is Earth's magnetic pulse.

Earthing and Grounding with Earth's Electromagnetic Field

Grounding the human body, also known as "earthing," refers to the practice of making direct physical contact with the earth's surface to allow the transfer of electrical energy from the earth into the body. In this process, the body also discharges static electricity back into the earth. Connecting the body to the earth enables free electrons from the earth's surface to spread over and into the body, where they have antioxidant effects.

Grounding appears to improve sleep, normalize the day-night cortisol rhythm, reduce pain, reduce stress, shift the autonomic nervous system from sympathetic toward parasympathetic activation, increase heart rate variability, speed wound healing, and reduce blood viscosity.

The concept is based on the idea that the earth carries a mild negative electric charge, and when a person makes contact with the earth (e.g., by walking barefoot on natural surfaces like soil, grass, or sand), electrons from the earth are transferred to the body, potentially reducing inflammation and improving overall well-being.

What is Schumann Resonance?

Schumann resonance is a natural electromagnetic frequency generated by Earth's magnetic field. It was discovered by German physicist Winfried Otto Schumann in 1952. Schumann was the first to predict the existence of these resonances in Earth's atmosphere.

Schumann resonance is a weak electromagnetic signal, having an amplitude of only a few microvolts per meter. This natural resonance is created by bouncing electromagnetic waves between the earth's surface and the ionosphere, forming a spherical waveguide.

Lightning strikes and solar flares further excite these frequencies, leading to a standing wave pattern in Earth's atmosphere. These frequencies fluctuate depending on geographical location, lightning, solar flares, atmospheric ionization, and daily cycles.

What Frequency is Schumann?

Schumann resonance is not a fixed frequency but an average number of global readings. Typically, the frequency of Schumann resonance is calculated by the distance between Earth's surface and the ionosphere.

The primary frequency of Schumann resonance is around 7.83 Hz and has several harmonic frequencies, including 14.07 Hz, 20.25 Hz, 26.41 Hz, and 32.45 Hz.

The frequency of 7.83 Hz has been called the heartbeat of Mother Earth. It is the prime broadcasting frequency for our body, mind, and cells. Every living thing on Earth is tuned to this frequency and its harmonics, making it the most crucial aspect of Earth's native electromagnetic fields in sustaining life. The DNA of all living beings on the planet has the capacity to resonate and receive the beneficial healing and relaxing effects of the Schumann resonance.

Does Schumann's Resonance Affect Humans?

Schumann resonance is critical for maintaining the balance and stability of Earth's electromagnetic environment. It is also linked to the normal functioning of the human brain and body.

The frequency of 7.83 Hz is the same as alpha brain waves. Alpha brain waves are very coherent and healing brain waves, which put us in a relaxed state called the Relaxation Response. This frequency helps us relax and deepen into healing processes and experience deep, healing sleep.

The frequency of 7.83 Hz is also the same as the frequency of infrared radiation, which has numerous healing effects on the human body.

All life uses this frequency as a fixed reference point to set the circadian clock. Modern living (surrounded by non-native EMFs and lighting) interrupts our connection to this frequency, and this throws our circadian rhythms off.

While research on the benefits of Schumann resonance is ongoing, multiple studies suggest that the Schumann frequency of 7.83 Hz positively affects human health and well-being. It has been linked to improved cognitive functions, reduced stress and anxiety, enhanced immune function, sleep function, and much more.

Research[1] has found that lack of exposure to Earth's magnetic field and the Schumann resonance was a significant contributing factor to symptoms such as fatigue, depression, bone loss, and sensations of weightlessness in astronauts returning from this space.

What Is the Difference Between Schumann Resonance and Grounding to the Earth?

Grounding to the earth and exposure to the Schumann resonance are two different concepts, although they both involve Earth's natural electromagnetic environment. Here's a breakdown of the differences between the two:

Grounding to the Earth

- Grounding, also known as earthing, refers to the practice of making direct physical contact with the earth's surface, typically by walking barefoot on the ground, sitting or lying on the earth, or using grounding devices that are electrically conductive.

- The primary purpose of grounding is to establish an electrical connection between your body and the earth, allowing for the transfer of free electrons from the earth's surface to your body. This process is believed to

---

1   https://www.brmi.online/post/2019/09/20/
    schumann-resonances-and-their-effect-on-human-bioregulation

have potential health benefits, as proponents suggest that it can help neutralize free radicals and reduce inflammation.

- Grounding is often associated with improving sleep, reducing stress, and promoting overall well-being. It is based on the idea that modern lifestyles often insulate us from direct contact with the earth's electrical charge, which may disrupt our natural electrical balance.

Exposure to Schumann Resonance

- The Schumann resonance, as mentioned earlier, is a set of extremely low-frequency electromagnetic waves that naturally occur in Earth's ionosphere. These waves are created by lightning discharges and are continuously present in Earth's atmosphere.

- Exposure to the Schumann resonance refers to the fact that these electromagnetic frequencies are constantly present in our environment. They are background radiation.

- To have exposure to the Schumann resonance, we need to get away from cities and power grids that interrupt these subtle frequencies.

In summary, grounding to the earth involves direct physical contact with the earth's surface to establish an electrical connection. Exposure to the Schumann resonance, on the other hand, pertains to the natural and constant presence of extremely low-frequency electromagnetic waves in our environment. The Schumann resonance is one mechanism that yokes our circadian clock to the cosmos. While both phenomena involve our relationship with Earth's electromagnetic environment, they are distinct practices with different objectives and scientific bases.

How Fabric Affects the Electricity of the Body and Grounding

The essay "Naked Beneath Your Clothing" by John Veltheim looks at how synthetic fibers interrupt the body's electrical system, or "wei chi" in traditional Chinese medicine, which alters comfort, cellular respiration, and temperature regulation.

Here is an excerpt from the essay:

> *Many interesting experiments have been done on the effect that clothing has on chi flow within the body. During the authors' years as Principal of the Brisbane College of Traditional Acupuncture and Natural Therapies in Australia, many experiments were conducted using highly sensitive equipment that could monitor and measure the flow of chi along the meridians. An acupuncture needle could be inserted into an acupuncture point to demonstrate the effect it has on the energy levels in other parts of the body along where that meridian flowed. For example, a needle inserted just below the knee at a point called stomach 36, would demonstrate an increased flow of energy along the whole stomach meridian running up the leg, through the stomach, up into the chest, and up to the eyes. Stimulating the needle can effectively help to balance, and heal, a stomach disorder (such as a stomach ulcer), or perhaps increase the energy flow to the eyes and improve vision.*

Some Interesting Experiments Demonstrated the Following

- When a patient was naked and had the needle stimulated, there was a measurable flow of energy—we'll call it 100 units.

- If that person then wore nylon underpants while this experiment was being done and the needle was being stimulated, the effective result of the flow was a reduction of energy flow of up to 60 percent.

- Repetitive experiments demonstrated that if a patient wore nylon underwear while receiving acupuncture treatments, that patient would need twice as many treatments to get the same results. Cotton underwear reduced the flow by 20 percent.

The Body as an Electrical Field

The surface of the skin is an electrical field that is constantly interacting with our environment and our inner body systems. The nervous system is another set of electrical circuits. The two combine to create varying electrical potentials that can easily be measured. This electrical potential is altered by the influence of different types of clothing. Synthetic clothing builds up a static charge on the body so that when a piece of metal is touched, the person gets a shock. Practitioners who work with bioenergetic therapy have found that static has detrimental effects on the body's electrical network, which, in turn, affects health.

Because the surface of the skin is an important circuit of piezo-electricity, this is how we connect with Schumann's resonance and Earth's electromagnetic field. Therefore, the clothes we wear should be of natural fiber, or we will be short-circuiting the body and not be able to absorb as much of the beneficial effects of our natural environment.

How Different Materials Affect Grounding

- **Conductive Shoe Soles.** If your shoe soles are made of conductive materials like leather, they can allow the flow of electrons between the earth and your body. When you walk on conductive surfaces like wet grass or moist soil wearing such shoes, you are more likely to maintain a connection to the earth's electric charge. This can facilitate grounding.

- **Non-Conductive Shoe Soles.** Shoes with non-conductive soles made of materials like plastic or insulating rubber can hinder the transfer of electrons between your body and the earth and prevent you from grounding.

- **Bare Feet and Natural Surfaces.** The most effective way to ground yourself is by walking barefoot on natural surfaces like soil, grass, and sand or even swimming in natural bodies of water. These surfaces are typically conductive and allow a direct connection to the earth's electric charge.

- **Grounding Mats and Products.** Some people use grounding mats or sheets, which are designed to be plugged into a grounded electrical outlet and connected to the body through a conductive fabric or wire. These products attempt to mimic the benefits of grounding when direct contact with the earth is not possible, such as in a building.

Dirty Energy in the Ground

However, all this said, there is another factor: the dirty electricity coming from the man-made power grid which is sent into the ground. This is measurable with a tri-field meter, and I have found it high even in some remote places. An ideal reading would be less than one volt per meter. Most areas in the US, even in remote mountain regions, are between four and nine. Because of that, I am not so sure grounding into the earth is even the wisest thing. It depends on where you are and who you are. Some EMF-sensitive people do better with the insulated synthetic pad when on the ground so they aren't grounding to the earth. This can be very confusing since the science is complex, and there are several opinions about how it works and what to do about it. It is probably best to use a closed-cell foam pad when backpacking, leaves piled up, or both. Get away from the ground a little bit… you are still in the Schumann's resonance when close to the ground.

Moving Outdoors — the Tipi Experiment

I wanted to see how all these theories actually worked in real life. After spending a few years testing these ideas out in various environments, from meadows to deep forests, mountain streams and waterfalls, mountaintops, deserts and prairies, I decided to move into a tipi using only natural fiber clothing and bedding.

I embarked on a journey, taking my first prototype wool sleeping bag and other natural fiber clothing and tents/tipi. My aim was to experiment with sleeping outdoors almost full-time.

Living Outside — My Daily Life

The results were undeniable. My sleep improved dramatically. The moment I lay down, I would relax instantly. I felt connected to Schumann's resonance, and it was as though I was "drinking" the air. The outside cold never bothered me, even when the temperature inches from my skin dropped below freezing. I remained alert, active, and engaged, both mentally and socially. From a biological standpoint, I realized that modern heating wasn't necessary. However, socially, it was challenging to maintain hygiene and appearance while balancing responsibilities between my outdoor and societal lives. Nonetheless, I resided in the tipi intermittently for three years, embracing the Paleolithic Philosophy to its extreme.

Physical Benefits

Living outdoors in the heart of winter was just the beginning. My daily life included walking or biking several miles to work and social events. Observing my counterparts, mostly my age or younger, they lived indoors and drove vehicles. To them, my lifestyle was alien.

Whenever I shared my experience, they responded with disbelief and fear. Some even said, "It makes me cold just to think about it." The underlying fear for many was that my theories might indeed be accurate. To get them to consider my perspective, I knew I had to prove my theories. Yet, even with evidence, many remained skeptical.

I developed a routine of greeting the sunrise and, several times a week would dive into the icy river when the air temperature was above 50 °F. Far from feeling run down, I adapted to the cold. Not only did my hands stop feeling numb, but I also noticed other health improvements. My metabolic rate increased, my eyesight improved, and my injuries healed faster.

The Results of My Experiment

Having used my body as a test subject for these theories, I am confident about their validity. I've since sought to replicate the results of my cold winter living experience in other settings.

Schumann's Resonance — the Earth's Natural Tuning Fork

Biological Attunement to the Planet's Frequency

The Schumann resonance acts as a natural tuning fork for our biological oscillators. Michael Hutchison, in his book *Mega Brain Power*, describes the 7.83 Hz frequency as one of the "window frequencies." This frequency has wide-ranging beneficial effects on humans, from enhanced healing to accelerated learning. When a biological system vibrates at this frequency, it is in resonance with the planet's magnetic frequency. This is considered the "natural electromagnetic matrix for all life on this planet, the frequency in which all life forms evolved, and, until recent decades, the dominant electromagnetic frequency in which all life took place."

Excerpts and Observations from Jack Kruse

How does Earth's electromagnetic field protect all life from EMF sources? The answer dates back to the Nobel Prize-winning physicist Richard Feynman's 1960s lectures on Earth's subtle energy sources:

- Earth's surface has an abundance of electrons, giving it a negative electrical charge.

- A person standing outside on a sunny day has an electrical charge difference between the earth and the top of their head due to insulators like shoes or flooring.

- Historically, life evolved connected to Mother Earth, allowing our brains to perceive the third dimension of time.

- Taking off one's shoes and making direct contact with the earth allows the earth's magnetic field to transmit through our bodies. This protective EMF pushes the voltage above our heads, shielding us from environmental EMF sources, including UV light and cosmic radiation.

Modern Disconnection from the Earth's Protective Shield

Until the arrival of modern man, all life had this protective shield. However:

- Exogenous EMFs that hit our bodies are canceled out by electrons supplied by the earth when we are grounded.

- Modern lifestyles have disconnected us from the earth, impacting our ability to synchronize biological reactions essential for life, such as ATP formation in the mitochondria.

- This disconnection causes energy leaks at our inner mitochondrial membrane, resulting in ATP production failure in positively charged environments.

- The role of energy is crucial for all life forms. Energy fuels every process that allows us to survive. A slow electron leak before death can cause diseases, and the inability to produce ATP results in death.

The Impact of Modern Life on Health

Few studies have addressed the effects of EMF. However, this lack of research is concerning due to:

- Global artificial EMF generation is now a trillion-dollar industry.

- Modern lifestyles impact our ability to maintain our circadian rhythm.

- The negative impact of artificial light and man-made EMFs on health, particularly on our mitochondria and telomeres.

The Connection Between Pineal Gland and Earth's Magnetic Field

Changes in Earth's magnetic field affect our Pineal Gland, impacting hormone production. For example:

- Melatonin, a vital neurohormone and cancer-suppressing agent, is not produced without the Schumann resonance in outer space.

- Melatonin production is also affected by electromagnetic pollution.

- All these clinical observations suggest a deep link between obesity and other diseases to an inflammatory condition.

- This inflammation is due to a lack of energy production in our cell's mitochondria, leading to a time contraction in the suprachiasmatic nucleus of the mammalian brain. Over time, this will cause illness.

Questions About Grounding and Sleep

Plastic vs. Natural Sleeping Mats

The question arose after observing pictures displaying both typical plastic insulation mattresses and the wool version. If a plastic layer is placed between the individual and the earth, won't it interrupt the positive grounding effects? Despite having a wool sleeping bag, the presence of such a mattress seems to disconnect one from the earth. Although there might be some connectivity through the air, the primary electricity seems to emanate from the ground.

Grounding Through Shoes

How does one ensure grounding through shoes? Is inserting a metal pin into the sole advisable? Or should one opt for an all-leather sole? There's also the concern of whether grounding shoes in environments with high EMF, like cities, are harmful due to the absorption of even more EMFs.

Response to Grounding Queries

Choice of Sleeping Surface

When sleeping outside in remote areas when not backpacking, I prefer the natural wool pad. Only during backpacking do I opt for the synthetic insulated closed-cell foam pad due to its weight and moisture considerations. While it does insulate from the earth's grounding effects, being within Schumann's resonance seems adequate for grounding purposes. Additional factors enhancing grounding include:

- Negative ions from trees.

- Mist, dew, fog, or mountain creek sprays.

- The cold's effect in minimizing the body's electron leakage.

Schumann resonance is currently the most effective grounding source, shielding us from harmful EMFs, both man-made and solar.

Materials like wood and leather are mildly conductive. They are favorable for grounding because they don't halt the electron flow like synthetic materials do.

Ground Condensation and Dirty Electricity

When grounding, it's essential to be wary of condensation on bedding materials from moisture, which can lead to mold if unattended. Practical solutions include using a slatted wooden bed frame, which can even be made in some places from poles found on-site, or constructing a bed with piled leaves covered by a tarp, which could be a synthetic or oil-clothed canvas for moisture protection.

However, dirty electricity from man-made power grids is another concern. This can be gauged with a voltmeter, with readings ideally being less than one volt per meter. Due to these EMF measurements, grounding into the earth might not always be the best choice. The suitability varies based on location and individual sensitivities. Some individuals, especially those sensitive to EMFs, might fare better with an insulated synthetic pad.

Shoes and Grounding

Grounding shoes may not be advisable due to the potential influx of dirty electricity. Walking barefoot occasionally is beneficial, but it's crucial to rely on personal instincts given the incomplete information available and the various factors in play.

Grounding Q and A

Question: Is it better to use a typical plastic insulation pad or a wool pad when backpacking?

Answer: When I am not backpacking, but am sleeping outdoors in a more permanent setup, I use the natural wool pad. If I am staying in a tipi or similar permanent camp, I use a wooden platform with a wool pad on top.

When backpacking, I use the synthetic insulated closed-cell foam pad for weight and moisture reasons. Always keep in mind your overall pack weight when choosing gear. An insulated pad reduces your pack weight versus a wool pad. And wool may absorb moisture and, therefore, doesn't lend itself to backpacking.

Question: Won't I lose the positive grounding effects when I put a plastic layer in between myself and the earth?

Answer: Yes, it does insulate away from the grounding effects of the earth. However, since one is still exposed to Schumann's resonance, there are still benefits similar to grounding.

In addition to that, there are negative ions in the air coming from the trees and oftentimes mist, dew, fog, or the spray of the mountain creeks. Consider the definition of grounding means adding electrons to the body, discharging static electricity, and increasing the Oxygen Reduction Potential (ORP) of the body.

The cold also has an additional effect of grounding by reducing the electron leakage of the body.

Also, when sleeping on a closed cell foam pad, to increase grounding, you can put a part of your body on the ground, such as letting the feet hang off the bottom and touch the ground. Some people use a three-quarter length pad instead of a full length.

Schumann's resonance is the best grounding source at this time, it seems. It protects us from harmful EMF radiation both from man-made sources as well as from the sun.

Testing with a Meter

Using a body voltage meter to determine if you are grounded involves measuring the electrical potential difference between your body and the ground. Here's a step-by-step guide on how to use a body voltage meter for this purpose:

Equipment Needed:

- **Body Voltage Meter.** Also known as a multimeter with body voltage measurement capability.

- **Grounding Mat or Sheet.** Optional, for ensuring a proper ground connection.

Steps:

1. Set Up the Meter
   1. Turn on the body voltage meter.

   2. Set it to measure AC voltage (usually denoted by a V with a wavy line).

2. Prepare the Ground Connection
   1. Ensure you have a good ground connection. You can use a grounding mat, sheet, or a grounding rod connected to the earth.

   2. If using a grounding mat or sheet, plug it into a grounded outlet or connect it to a grounding rod.

3. Connect Yourself to the Ground (optional for reference)

   1. Stand or sit on the grounding mat or sheet. Alternatively, touch a grounded object (e.g., a metal water pipe connected to the ground).

4. Measure the Voltage

   1. Hold the body voltage meter in one hand.

   2. Use the other hand to hold the sensor/probe of the meter, or attach it to your skin using an adhesive electrode if provided.

   3. If the meter has a second probe, connect it to a true ground (like a grounded outlet or grounding rod).

5. Read the Measurement

   1. While standing or sitting away from any grounding source, take a reading. This will be your body voltage when not grounded.

   2. Note the voltage reading displayed on the meter.

6. Check Grounding Effectiveness

   1. Now, connect yourself to the grounding source (grounding mat, sheet, or grounded object).

   2. Take another reading with the meter while you are connected to the ground.

   3. Compare the two readings.

Interpreting the Results

- **Not Grounded.** If you are not grounded, the body voltage meter will show a higher voltage, typically reflecting the voltage induced by surrounding electrical fields (usually between 1–10 volts or more).

- **Grounded.** When you are grounded, the voltage reading should drop significantly, ideally to a very low value close to 0 volts. This indicates that the electrical potential difference between your body and the ground is minimal, confirming that you are grounded.

Tips

- Ensure that the grounding mat or sheet is properly connected to a true ground.

- Perform the measurements in different locations to check the consistency of grounding effectiveness.

- Make sure you are away from electronic devices and power sources while taking initial measurements to avoid interference.

By following these steps, you can effectively use a body voltage meter to determine if you are properly grounded.

Question: Should I ground my shoes?

A similar question arises with shoes. How do you ground yourself with shoes? Do you put a metal pin in the sole, or do you have a recommendation for an all-leather sole? And might it even be bad to ground your shoes in heavy EMF, e.g., in the city, because you pick up even more EMFs?

Answer: Sense your body's response. When in natural areas, I walk barefoot when I can. In urban areas, this may not be a good idea due to the dirty electricity that is in the ground from the electrical power grid. I think we need to use our instincts often because there is a lot of unclear information and multiple factors to consider. I would not try to make my shoes grounded for that reason, as well. It is a waste of time and possibly counterproductive.

Question: What about other natural materials like wood or leather?

Answer: Leather and wood are natural materials that are mildly conductive. This means that they can indeed help ground the body to the earth. Wearing leather moccasins is excellent for grounding. However, I haven't found a moccasin that holds up well in wet conditions. Furthermore, there is an issue with lack of traction because moccasins can be slippery.

CHAPTER 3

Reevaluating Choices

When getting into the spirit of rewilding, we need to think carefully about what we would like to let go of and leave behind. Are there things we are bringing into nature that interrupt a deeper connection and experience? What are some of the problems with modern camping, and some things we should avoid if we choose the path of rewilding?

How We Sabotage Going into Nature Without Realizing It

Many people have a feeling of wanting to connect more deeply with nature. And yet, in the modern world, the art of being in nature has taken a strange twist. People often go camping and bring the city with them in many ways. The modern outdoor camping adventure often leaves little room to actually experience the silence and direct connection to the source that humans had before the Industrial Revolution. "Glamping," for example, involves bringing luxuries from home and creating an urban settlement for the weekend in a natural place. And modern backpacking has become an arena in which companies compete to outdo one another with the latest NASA-developed gear and fabric that will allow us to be in nature. However, oftentimes, this state-of-the-art gear and fabric intended to take us into nature end up cutting off our natural biological processes and adding more toxins to our already overburdened bodies. We are yearning for nature, but we have lost the art of actually connecting with nature.

> *We are yearning for nature, but we have lost the*
> *art of actually connecting with nature.*

When we are hiking, camping, and backpacking, we are outdoors in the perfect opportunity to practice rewilding. In fact, most people would think that as long as you are outdoors you are rewilding no matter what. Right? Well, it depends....

The funny thing is, it is easier to rewild your home than it is to rewild your outdoor gear and experience. There are many self-sabotaging practices of the modern outdoorsy person that they are completely unaware of. What do I mean by self-sabotaging practices? Things we do that weaken our bodies.

It's when you go outside that you especially need your body to work well. It is just you and nature; you and the rain, wind, cold, heat, bugs, snakes, and sun. Our bodies need to be rewilded in order to go into nature and withstand the rigors presented. That's why my philosophy is that the body is the first piece of gear. Because if our bodies are nutrient-deficient and full of toxins, we won't be able to handle everyday outdoor things like sun, cold, bugs, moving on uneven terrain, etc. A strong, robust body will be able to handle temperature extremes and sun exposure and even ward off insects to a point. Your body is your sacred vehicle and temple.

However, the outdoor industry has over-domesticated camping. In civilization, machines and chemicals can do the work, and we can hide behind them. But when it's just you against bare nature, that's where the buck stops.

Rewilding is about blending, harmonizing, merging, and interacting with nature. However, the approach of modern camping is often to bring along the flawed Western paradigm that nature is dangerous, and we need to conquer it and keep it at a distance. Of course, this is mostly subconscious. And there is nothing wrong with whatever ways people want to enjoy the outdoors. However, going hiking and camping represents our one chance to have a primordial experience, and we blow it by wrapping ourselves in plastic, breathing and slathering our bodies with toxic chemicals to keep the sun or bugs away, and eating foods that don't support healthy adaptation to the outdoors. Following are ten ways people—without meaning to—sabotage their outdoor adventures.

Self-Sabotaging Practices of Outdoor Enthusiasts

- **Wearing sunglasses.** Sunglasses block the beneficial rays of the sun necessary for proper melatonin production and the balancing of circadian rhythms. The need to wear sunglasses is also an indication of a lack of minerals needed to use our eyes better in glare environments.

- **Synthetic gear.** Some synthetic tents and other gear off-gas chemicals full of endocrine-disrupting phytoestrogens. These accumulate in our bodies and create a "body burden," which gradually destroys health. (There are a couple of new fabrics that are safe even though they are synthetic, which will be discussed later.)

- **Synthetic clothing and bedding.** Synthetic clothing and bedding disrupt our bodies' release of moisture and temperature regulation, as well as unground us and rob electrons from our bodies.

- **Standard hard-soled and padded shoes** with heels and arches cause our foot muscles to atrophy and also create structural imbalances in the entire body. They can cause many foot problems as well as knee and back pain and throw off our gait, causing inefficient movement patterns and biomechanics.

- **Bug spray.** The use of bug spray with endocrine-disrupting toxic chemicals harms health. Regardless of the dosage, DEET should be treated as a hazardous chemical. It can cause reactions to the skin and neurological system. DEET is quickly absorbed into the bloodstream through application to the skin (absorption from 20–80 percent), and while many people can use it without incident, others experience severe side effects. It is linked to causing seizures in children. Long-term use in adults is linked to impaired cognitive function, insomnia, and mood disturbances. These chemicals enter the body through the skin. DEET is also a solvent and can dissolve plastics and synthetic fabrics. Unfortunately, this includes the synthetic, moisture-wicking clothing backpackers typically wear, such as polyester, nylon, and spandex, as well as backpacking gear, including sunglasses, tents, canopies, sleeping bags, camera cases, and backpacks.

- **Diet.** The standard backpacker's diet is demineralized, overprocessed, and contains little, if any, healthy fats. This disrupts our hormones, circadian rhythms, and our body's ability to generate heat. Long term, this diet leads to deficiencies and demineralizes the body with its anti-nutrients such as lectins, phytates, and oxalates.

- **Overexertion.** Overexertion depletes our glycogen reserve and cellular energy. Leave the ego in the city and walk according to your current fitness level. Hiking and especially backpacking are going to put more demands on the body than just about anything. This exercise will mobilize toxins into the bloodstream, and too much can be painful and damaging. Start slow, go to your edge, rest when needed, and build up according to what your body can handle. Of course, it is also necessary to train before embarking on a trek, and more will be discussed about how to do this.

- **Chairs and air mattresses.** These props often put the body in unnatural positions, which hurt alignment and breathing, thus cutting off vitality. We need to learn how to comfortably get in positions when there are no props and use aligned body mechanics. Learning and practicing healthy primal movements at home, such as crawling, squatting, sitting on the floor, etc., will adapt you to the new environment, which is devoid of the furniture we have become accustomed to. It's not about being uncomfortable, but it is about using the body in ways that put us in multiple healthy positions rather than the few static positions of our over-domesticated world.

- **Soft plastic water bladders and excessive water consumption.** Drinking from toxic plastic water bladders adds to our chemical body burden. The idea of drinking excessive water is also another concern. While dehydration needs to be avoided, drinking too much water can lead to loss of electrolytes. You can add salt to the water to help against this. The amount of water to drink varies with many factors. I do use plastic water bottles, but these are hard plastic, and the water doesn't stay in the bottle very long before it is used.

- **Flashlights.** Flashlights are a form of artificial blue light. Any time we are exposed to artificial blue light at night, our circadian rhythms and melatonin production are disrupted, reducing the quality of sleep and leading to less energy the next day. The answer is to use a flashlight with a red color option. Using a red light at night is the way to go. Candles and fires are also great since they emit only the red part of the light spectrum.

- **Suntan lotion.** This is full of toxic chemicals that enter your body, increasing the toxic body burden. The alternative is sun-protective clothing and some kind of animal fat or body butter.

Preparing the Body for Backpacking

Your Body — Your First Piece of Gear

Rewilding for a backpacking trip starts long before the trip itself. This is because the first piece of gear for a backpacking trip is actually your body. If we consider how biology interacts with the environment, from there, we can see what kind of gear best supports that interaction. Being outside in nature can be a part of a healing journey, but also one needs to be at a certain level of health before starting. Hiking with a loaded pack in rough terrain can be very rigorous, and this exertion can cause the dumping of toxins such as oxalates, heavy metals, and more. When this happens, it is often called a "healing crisis" and can include symptoms such as soreness, fatigue, headaches, insomnia, and aches and pains in general. Because of this, some people will need to build health first and go slow and short distances. Many of us are recovering from toxic exposures to mold or other issues. So sometimes, it begins with building health through diet, remineralization, detoxing, rest, and perhaps simple camping without a backpack. Backpacking can be used as part of the healing journey if we go slow and listen to our body. It can also be considered a goal to attain and considered the fruit of our healing efforts put into use.

Whether you are ready to begin your hike or you are building up to it, you want to know the proper clothing and other gear that optimizes the healing effects of nature. There is a saying in the outdoor world, "There is no such thing as bad weather, only bad gear." So we want clothing, tents, and bedding that allow the natural process of moisture and heat exchange and regulation rather than those that hinder or block the process. Another way to prepare the body is with the right training, cold adapting, and building health through diet. Backpacking can be approached as an extreme sport where you challenge yourself to cover as many miles as possible, or it can be approached as a way to practice forest bathing, which is more of a spa experience. And these can be combined as well.

PART 2

Getting Geared Up

CHAPTER 4

Natural vs. Synthetic Fabrics

← ——— «

THE STORY OF A BACKPACKING TREK IN LINWOOD GORGE

THIS STORY SHOWS REWILDED BACKPACKING GEAR BEING USED IN A VARIETY OF SITUATIONS.

Not long before sunset, I pull into a remote trailhead intersection along a windy road to drop my car off. I see some guys standing there, and I ask if they are with the Backpacking Meetup group, and they are. We introduce ourselves, and soon, the leader arrives. We arrange our backpacks in one car and then pile in to carpool several miles to the starting point of our trip. From there, we will hike our way back over the next four days. The Linville Gorge Wilderness area is not far from my home in Pisgah National Forest in Western North Carolina. We whiz by miles of wild forest along the curvy road as we chat about the upcoming itinerary. It is November, and the sky is getting dark quickly.

Since I was fourteen years old, I have been going through a process of becoming more deeply connected to and integrated with nature on many levels—a process that was later termed "rewilding." Rewilding myself and life had brought about many profound inner and outer transformations and had saved my health. For the past several years,

I had also transformed and reinvented—rewilded—my backpacking gear and clothing, as well as much of what I was bringing inside my backpack. I had become captivated with natural fibers and rediscovered how to incorporate them into my outdoor gear. I had designed and sewn my own backpack, sleeping bag, and clothing. My shoes were "minimalist," which meant there was a very thin, quarter-inch-thick sole and no support or heel. I also created recipes for the optimal nutrient-dense, energizing foods to bring on a backpacking trip and designed other components of my gear, such as an herbal first aid kit.

I jumped at the chance to join this four-day backpacking trip with a backpacking enthusiast's Meetup Group so that I could test my gear and ideas for the first time with other backpackers who were using modern gear. I had gone on a few trips before, but this was the first trip I would be going with a group with my new gear. And now the day has arrived. The day to test everything I had created.

For me, the primary objective of this trip, besides just having an amazing time, is to put my gear and theories under rigorous tests and scrutiny without any hidden agenda to prove anything in particular (maintaining the neutral observer stance of a scientist). With my intense curiosity, I need to see just what parts of the results of my intensive rewilding journey will work and what won't when juxtaposed against other campers using the latest advanced technologies for camping and backpacking. I also just want to go out with a group that knows some routes I am not familiar with and to have the camaraderie and safety of companions.

I pull out my light green canvas backpack. With mild weather I decide to hike in shorts, so I change into them and put my waxed cotton pants inside the pack. After a little more adjusting of my shoes and the straps on my pack, I walk over to the group. People have slick, bright-colored packs and jackets, hats, and clothes made out of synthetic materials. Teal, bright red, and dark blue. At one time, I had also been a gear junkie and on top of the latest trends. I am not exactly sure how my techniques and gear will measure up to the standards of modern backpacking. Will it work the way I claim it worked? Will it stand up to the elements? Will it protect me and my things from possible rain, cold, wind, and heat?

When you're the only one saying something, and you are convinced it works, but the world has yet to recognize it and continues to be skeptical, well, that's a very tough place to be. You start to ask yourself if you are just deluding yourself.

We weigh our packs. Everyone's pack is pretty close to thirty pounds, including food and water. Mine is almost exactly thirty pounds, so I am very pleased it is comparable to the pack weight of others in the group. So far, so good. We have to bear in mind (pardon the pun) that weight isn't the only thing that matters. In fact, there will be several tests my gear will be going through on this trip:

- Overall pack weight.

- Overall functionality of gear when faced with weather extremes such as rain, cold, wind, etc.

- Carrying not too much and not too little of anything (such as water, food, etc.). Overall comfort and enjoyment of the experience. (For instance, even if a pack is light, is the person still warm and well-fed and able to adjust to the changing conditions found in nature?)

- Having everything you need. Not leaving an important item out. Being prepared for emergencies such as first aid and survival items.

I'm not sure how my pack is so close in weight to these other modern backpacker's packs because my sleeping bag and clothes are quite a bit heavier. When packing, I must have saved in other areas in order to make up for the discrepancy, but I'm not sure exactly what areas are different. My sleeping bag weighs four pounds, compared to the average down bag, which weighs about one to two pounds or less.

We all have about the same amount of food by weight (eight pounds or two pounds per day). I suspect my super-efficient, two-pound, rustic tent/shelter is partly what made my pack lighter. And it will look primitive; however, it will outperform their modern tents by miles.

When I stepped out of the car at seven that evening, I had already been strengthening my body internally and building my body through eating certain foods and moving in certain ways in my day-to-day life. All of these choices and changes I had undertaken in my life meant my body would have the strength to endure possible unexpected challenges and also would simply give me more happiness and joy through feeling healthy, energetic, and strong on the trip.

It is twilight now. The glow of the sunset has faded, and the sky is dark blue. Loaded with packs, we trod away from the parking lot, heading into the forest. We will be night hiking for a couple of miles along a trail that climbs the east rim of Shortoff Mountain. A moist, unseasonal, summer-like wind blows as we carefully step over and around objects along the trail. Lights from nearby towns glow faintly in the distance. Stopping from time to time to soak in the alluring silence, we often catch views of Lake James, which mostly appears as a massive black zone with no lights right below us. We have all donned our headlamps, which light the way in front of us. I don't like using light at night because this destroys one's night vision as well as circadian rhythms, which also interrupts quality sleep. But I use my flashlight with the red setting. This makes it more difficult to navigate but saves the eyes from the brightness.

Linville Gorge is the deepest and perhaps most rugged gorge in the eastern United States. Nicknamed the Grand Canyon of the East, the Cherokee called it "Eeseeoh," meaning "river of many cliffs," a reference to the many vertical rock outcroppings that line the gorge. Many years ago, Cherokee people walked along the trails we are walking on now, surrounding "Eeseeoh."

As we walk deeper into the forest, our bodies shed modern electromagnetic burdens, and our lungs breathe in unpolluted air filled with oxygen, plant aromatics, and negative ions. This creates deeper relaxation and boosts health, creating such effects as stronger immunity and more power to detoxify. As we walk, our bodies move in new ways in relation to the stones and contours of the trail, using different muscles, stretches, and ways of balancing than when on flat floors and sidewalks. We connect more and more to Earth, absorbing Earth's energy and magnetic field.

When stepping into nature, we are allowing the body to shed various stressors from modern times and to return to states of being experienced by our ancient ancestors. In a way, we are going not only through space but through time.

We finally make it to the campsite, which is a nice flat area with tall trees spread far enough apart to give a spacious feeling. I plop my heavy pack onto the ground and start pulling out the gear. First, I set up my open-air tarp by finding two trees about ten feet apart. A cord gets attached to each tree to support the ridgeline of the tarp, and then the sides get staked down. Once I have my shelter erected, I pull out the ground cloth and place it underneath. Then I put my pack with the rest of my clothes and gear inside as well. We all walk around to gather firewood, crunching through the leaves, occasionally making a loud crack sound, breaking sticks. Soon, we have a nice fire that flickers and rises upwards, crackling and throwing orange embers into the dark. The firelight makes the trunks of the surrounding trees rosy light gray. We are each tending to our supper, which mostly consists of heating water to add some kind of instant meal to it like noodles or rice. I take out my homemade pemmican, which is a Native American power-packed food consisting of dried and pulverized grass-fed beef, which is mixed with rendered fat and berry powder. I had heard of this food for many years before I finally found enough information about how to make it. I thought it would make the ultimate backpacking food, and I was right! It is similar in nutrition to eating a fresh steak; however, this is something that is light and compact enough to carry on the trail and requires no refrigeration. The

Native Americans were the ultimate backpackers! While others are fixing mostly carbohydrate-based foods lacking in nutrient density, I am enjoying a delicious and hearty meal that is practically effortless. I also heat up some powdered bone and mushroom broth and eat it sitting as we chat about the day's adventure.

As we sit around the fire, stars flicker here and there, peeking through past the cloud cover above. The campfire dies down to big, fat, red, glowing chunks, and a chill in the air finds us. We've finished dinner. The forest shadows, hushed but full of the life of the night, beckon to our dreams.

I crawl into my wool sleeping bag and pull the soft wool scarf around my head and face. The wool is soft and calming the way it seems to be just the right temperature. It provides a sense of containment even when sleeping out in the open, allowing my body to slip into deep relaxation. The peace of the still ground and quiet trees leads me into dreamtime.

Day 2

We wake up to temperatures around 50 °F and the dreaded rain pounding on our tents. I'm somewhat elated because I really want to test my gear to the max. Will my wool and waxed cotton clothing and sleeping bag live up to the claims I am making?

Day two was going to turn out to be strenuous and windy. I briefly review the agenda:

Day 2 (Saturday 11/23)
Details: Sunrise at 7:11.

- Continue for a couple of miles of relatively flat terrain along the east rim.

- Begin the descent on the MST (Mountains-to-Sea Trail) into Chimney Gap around the 4-mile mark. Reach Chimney Gap (5.8 mi.).

- Water can be found by following a trail to the west about 1000' down to the head of Chimney Branch (10 min). Trail is unmarked and can be found behind the campsite on the west side.

- From Chimney Gap, follow the MST on the ascent to The Chimneys. This climb is strenuous and gains over 1000' in 1 mi.

- The Chimneys is a craggy playground of stone boulders, pillars, and caves. This is a good place to enjoy lunch (if you carry up water) and explore with spectacular views of the eastern Piedmont, the gorge itself, and the Black Mountains.

- Now the MST descends a bit to the Table Rock parking area, and after another 0.25 mi., forks right to continue on the MST (side trail to ascend Table Rock Mountain in another 100 yd.) or left takes you on the Little Table Rock Trail.

We have breakfast in the rain as we discuss the day's plans, and then we go to our tents to pack up. I need to decide what I will wear versus what I will protect and need later. I know that whatever I wear may become completely soaked.

Clothing That I Put On My Body

- One layer of merino base layer for top and bottom (base layer)

- One pair of wool socks

- Leather minimalist boots

- Waxed cotton pants (shell layer) and

- Waxed cotton parka (shell layer)

- Wool finger gloves

- Merino headwrap on my head

- Wide-brimmed wool felt hat

Clothing and Gear That I Put in the Waterproof Silnylon Stuff Sack in My Backpack

- Lucky Sheep™ Rewilder Wool Sleeping Bag (four pounds)

- Wool sweater (two pounds)

- One set merino base layer

- Two pairs of wool socks

The rest of my pack is exposed to the rain. My food, cooking kit, and first aid kit are wrapped in Ziplock bags and can get wet. My tent and the ground cloth are already wet and packed in the outside pockets of the backpack. I put my lunch, water, and alcohol stove fuel in an outside pocket. That is about all the gear I have with me.

We start out on the muddy trail as water sloshes into our boots. I feel myself getting wetter and colder with each step. This, our second day hiking on a four-day trip, is what most people would call a miserable day.

So, as we're slogging through the rain and mud, let's talk about gear. You may have noticed that I'm wearing wool, cotton, and other natural fibers. What is the difference between natural versus synthetic fibers when it comes to backpacking and rewilding? Much of modern gear is made of synthetic fibers. Let's first look at the characteristics and performance of synthetic fibers.

Story to be continued…

On Our Skin — Fabrics, Textiles, and Fibers

A few years ago, I had a strange fascination with sleeping outside. I wanted to find a way to make my camping experience better. I didn't like how everything seemed like a compromise to make gear lightweight and utilitarian. I wanted to adapt my body to the wild outdoors so that I was actually living in it and not merely camping in it. "Camping" implies compromise, temporary, portable, just getting by. I wanted to consider my expeditions as "living" outdoors rather than camping. That meant being at ease in all different circumstances: rain, snow, summer, and everything in between. It just made sense because nature has all the elements for living.

Question for Contemplation

What would it be like to go on a "living in nature"
trip rather than a "camping" trip?

I started looking at what ways camping gear may be causing discomfort or compromise in what could be a more sensuous experience. For example, there are many factors outdoors that enhance sleep, such as the Schumann resonance, invigorating exercise, the sun, fresh air, and being away from everyday duties. But people tend to think of their bed at home as superior for quality sleep than where they sleep when camping. So, what is essentially different as far as sleeping at home versus camping? And why do people idealize their own bed as the most comfortable place to sleep?

The gear I was finding on the market was becoming a roadblock to my progress. At this time, I had also become sick with Multiple Chemical Sensitivities and could no longer use my toxic-covered-in-chemicals modern camping gear. I had to figure out a new way.

It was almost by accident when I first learned about the power of wool to not only increase vitality but also raise the comfort level of winter. It was at a time (late 1990s) when I was well aware the outdoor community was adopting synthetics as the new best thing to stay warm. I, too, had turned my wardrobe into mostly synthetic. I happened to find a nice-looking wool sweater at a thrift store, and when I put it on, I felt a different kind of comfort. It had been a few years since I had worn wool, and so I noticed the difference. Something about wool went deeper. That experience turned me around, even before I heard anyone talk about wool. It was almost impossible to find wool at the time since the world had pretty much thrown the baby out with the bathwater in search of the newest and latest. Then, I did some research and found the science behind how wool works versus synthetics.

Over the next few years, I learned how to sew and designed a wool sleeping bag and organic canvas tent. I slept most nights outdoors because I was trying to understand the dynamics of how to live in the cold. I know; it sounds crazy. But I was fascinated with how this new sleeping arrangement was affecting me. I would go on wilderness excursions, taking my ragtag natural gear prototypes (I had barely learned to sew at the time) and would spend a few days doing what came to be known as Forest Bathing. Forest Bathing is when we go into nature with the goal of rejuvenation and sensory experience rather than accomplishment.

And Slowly, My Equipment Evolved...
The first and biggest elephant in the closet is the fact that the clothing, tents, and sleeping bags are synthetic.

Synthetic Fibers
Our world has become ubiquitously synthetic. There are fake foods, fake news, fake people, and artificial everything, including fibers. Almost everything we wear, touch, and sleep with is synthetic fiber.

This has come about in the last thirty years due to the rising tide of the synthetic fiber industry. Slowly, old traditional fabrics such as silk, cotton, linen, hemp, and wool have been replaced with cheaper manmade products such as nylon and polyester variations. When we zip ourselves up inside a synthetic sleeping bag (even down fill uses synthetic fiber) and inside a synthetic tent (and usually wearing synthetic clothing), we have effectively wrapped ourselves in three layers of plastic. And yet, you will find few alternatives for lightweight backpacking and camping in the outdoor stores.

Complete natural fiber backpacking clothing: minimalist barefoot shoes, merino scarf and hat, merino base layer bottoms, beeswax canvas parka, wool felted mittens, wool pants, alpaca sweater, merino base layer tops, alpaca socks.

Problems with Synthetic Fibers

Wool to Solve Getting Too Wet and Cold During Winter Camping

> *"I was on a trip in the Sierras and experienced what I call 'synthetic hell.' I was wearing wet plastic clothes inside a wet plastic bag inside a tiny wet plastic tent, all in 25-degree weather with 14" of snow on top. Case study claustrophobia. Gave up and walked all night, 19 miles in the snow to shelter. I'm throwing all that crap away and starting over with a more natural system."* ~Testimonial from a Lucky Sheep™ customer

Toxic Chemicals

Toxic chemicals with potential health and environmental impacts are widely used in the manufacture of outdoor clothing and gear, according to a Greenpeace study. The environmental activist group found traces of poly- and perfluorinated compounds (PFCs) in thirty-six of forty products they tested, according to the results found at www.detox-outdoor.org.

Chemicals such as perfluorooctane sulfonate (PFOS) and perfluorooctanoic acid (PFOA) are used to make moisture-wicking and water-repellent equipment, including jackets, pants, sleeping bags, boots, and tents. The compounds help keep campers and hikers dry and dirt-free, but they are hazardous to the environment and human health, Greenpeace says. The chemicals are also widely used in common household items such as non-stick cooking utensils and fire-retardant foam.

Ungrounding (Skin Cells Can't Breathe, Lose Energy)

In addition to the toxic chemicals, there is another way synthetic fabrics create a state of inflammation in the body. Because they contain metals (built into the petroleum molecule), synthetics short-circuit the electrical flow along our skin, called piezoelectricity. This increases the static charge of our body, which ungrounds us and causes us to lose electrons. Essentially, we breathe through our skin. Synthetics block that process. (Our skin can't absorb negative ions from the air, which is one of the primary healing effects of being in nature.)

Moisture Trapping and Heat Regulation

Due to the fact that synthetic fabric traps moisture and heat next to the skin, the heart has to pump faster in an effort to adjust body temperature. When the heart beats significantly faster, both at night while sleeping as well as during the day, the sleep cycle is interrupted because the brain waves cannot relax into their natural pattern. The result is waking up not feeling fully refreshed because you didn't experience the full sleep cycle. Most people attribute this discomfort to the fact they are camping and not in the comfortable bed they are used to.

The Synthetic Tent

Besides the clothing and bedding, the other piece of synthetic gear presenting issues is the tent. The problems with the tent are actually similar to those of the sleeping bag.

The synthetic tent:

- Holds your body's perspiration and breath in, making the air damp and clammy and

- Keeps the fresh, rejuvenating air with healing biocides and terpenes out.

I find sleeping under the open sky is the ultimate. The next best thing is an open-air tarp, which allows air circulation through the front and back. There is nothing like getting a super dose of fresh air and negative ions to create sleep like nothing else. When camping in ways other than backpacking, I like to use a canvas tent, which breathes through the fabric, for optimal ventilation.

Pros and cons of synthetic vs. canvas tents:

Canvas	Synthetic
Breathability	
Humidity is the most critical factor in environmental comfort. Unlike synthetics, canvas allows small moisture particles from breath, sweat, and cooking to escape.	Non-breathable vapor-impermeable fabric prevents moisture from sweat and breath from escaping. High humidity means sweat won't evaporate, making it feel even hotter inside than outside.
Warm in Cold Weather	
Canvas tents hold some heat in from the ground keeping you warmer during chilly weather.	Plastic builds up humidity making you colder and has scant insulating ability.
Cool in Hot Weather	
Canvas allows air to pass through it making it the tent of choice in the tropics and summer. Pitch the Crystal Moon Tent six or more inches off the ground for 360-degree ventilation.	Synthetic tents are stifling during hot weather since the only ventilation is that from mesh netting.
Durability	
Canvas is tough, rip resistant, and repairable. Pre-treated and re-treatable, a properly maintained canvas tent can last for years.	Ripping and tearing easily, synthetic fabric is nearly impossible to repair. Although cheap to buy, any damage can mean a ruined trip and a total tent replacement.
UV Resistance	
Quality canvas has a protective treatment to withstand sun damage and can be easily retreated to maintain that protection for years to come.	Damaging UV rays degrade synthetic fabric quickly while canvas endures. Once weakened, plastic fibers are prone to breakage and aftermarket treatments can do little to prolong the life of the tent.
Wind Resistance	
The conical design, robust canvas, and sturdy steel stakes stands up to high winds, driving rain, and blowing snow.	Poles with a smaller diameter than a Slurpee straw, a thin plastic tent membrane, and miniature aluminum stakes simply don't do the job when you need them most.

Canvas	Synthetic
Toxicity	
Organic canvas coated with beeswax is as good as it gets…no VOCs, PBDEs, flame retardants, or phthalates at all.	Many synthetic tents off gas toxic endocrine disrupting chemicals and are also a fire hazard. Silnylon and Cuben Fiber are fairly non-toxic.
Rain Shedding	
Rain causes the fibers of the canvas to swell. The surface tension of a raindrop prevents the water from passing through the tight weave of quality canvas, keeping you dry, naturally.	Plastics do not absorb water well. Initially rain will shed, but after the fabric has been saturated it can hold moisture and further limit breathability, increasing humidity, making the inside feel damp.
Weight	
Canvas is heavy and gets heavier when wet.	Synthetic wins out. Best place for synthetic tents is backpacking where they are a necessity. The best choice for optimal ventilation is an open-ended tarp which is very light and practical.

We Want Maximum Exposure to Air

Some of the plausible pathways from contact with nature to improved health stem from specific environmental conditions.

1. Natural environments contain chemical and biological agents with known health implications. Many plants give off phytoncides (antimicrobial volatile organic compounds), which reduce blood pressure, alter autonomic activity, and boost immune functioning, among other effects.[2]

---

2   Komori et al., (1995). Effects of citrus fragrance on immune function and depressive states. *Neuroimmunomodulation* 2 174–180; Dayawansa et al. (2003). Autonomic responses during inhalation of natural fragrance of Cedrol in humans. *Auton. Neurosci.* 108 79–86; Li et al. (2006). Phytoncides (wood essential oils) induce human natural killer cell activity. *Immunopharmacol. Immunotoxicol.* 28 319–333.

2. The air in forested and mountainous areas and near moving water contains high concentrations of negative air ions,[3] which reduce depression,[4] among other effects.

3. These environments also contain mycobacterium vaccae, a microorganism that appears to boost immune functioning.[5] Similarly, environmental biodiversity has been proposed to play a key role in immune function via its effects on the microorganisms living on the skin and in the gut, although the evidence for this is mixed.

Exploring Tent Alternatives

The first tent alternative I designed was a beeswax-coated canvas. This tent allows air to pass through it both ways. So, it will release moisture generated by the body, and it will allow fresh air inside. It is very strange, almost magic-like, how the rain will penetrate through the surface but not fall down. You can see the water flowing down the inside of the tent, but you still don't get wet! This tent was okay for a little forest bathing but not practical for actual backpacking because it becomes extremely heavy when wet.

Further research led me to Ray Jardine, an early pioneer of lightweight backpacking and author of *Trail Life*. I made a "Ray's Way" backpacking tarp from a lightweight synthetic fabric called silnylon. He believes closed tents are not good for the same reasons I do (lack of

---

3   Li et al. (2010). A day trip to a forest park increases human natural killer activity and the expression of anti-cancer proteins in male subjects. *J. Biol. Regul. Homeost. Agents* 24 157–165.

4   Terman et al. (1998). A controlled trial of timed bright light and negative air ionization for treatment of winter depression. *Arch. Gen. Psychiatry* 55 875–882; Goel et al. (2005). Controlled trial of bright light and negative air ions for chronic depression. *Psychol. Med.* 7 945–955.

5   Lowry et al. (2007). Identification of an immune-responsive mesolimbocortical serotonergic system: potential role in regulation of emotional behaviour. *Neuroscience* 146 756–772.

ventilation). His tarp design (which is from an old-time design orig-inally made from canvas) is open on each end and optionally open on the sides, depending on how you pitch it. Jardine's philosophy is that moisture from the body needs to escape using this kind of ventilation. He believes comfort and temperature regulation are best achieved by having some wind and air pushing through the tent/tarp rather than by sealing everything up. He also, like me, likes the feeling of being connected to the surroundings rather than zipped up and sealed off.

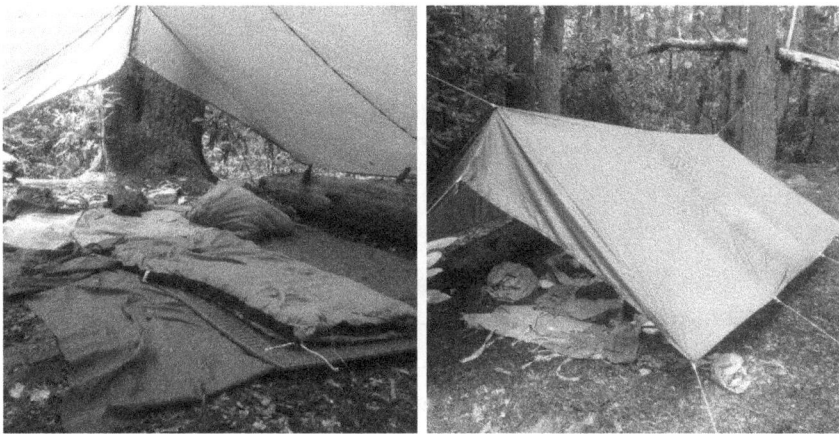

Open air tarp weighs 2 lbs. and fits two people.

When sealed up in a plastic tent, we are cut off from the fresh air full of all the aromas of the trees and flowers, negative ions from the mist of the creeks, and negative ions in the air from dew, fog, and rain. The forest, prairie, or desert air is healing, so a tent or tarp that allows us to experience it fully will provide the best sleep. For example, research shows that trees do have healing powers. For one thing, they release antimicrobial essential oils, called phytoncides, that protect them from germs and have a host of health benefits for people. These tree oils boost mood and immune system func-tion; reduce blood pressure, heart rate, stress, anxiety, and confusion; improve sleep and creativity; and may even help fight cancer and depression. These and other impressive benefits of forest medicine are cataloged by Dr. Qing Li, chairman of the Japanese Society of Forest Medicine, in his book *Forest Bathing*. These healing and sensuous aspects of nature are part of the reason we are going out in nature in the first place, so it's important not to prevent ourselves from experiencing them.

Not only are we cut off from all these "food for the body and soul" parts of nature around the tent, but the sealed-up, synthetic tent also traps our own body's moisture—breath and sweat—inside with us (we release two liters per night in breath and insensible perspiration). There are many reasons to rethink the tent design.

Moisture Wicking Fabrics

Synthetics can also be called "plastic" since they are the same petroleum molecule and behave the same way as plastic. Synthetic windbreakers trap the moisture that gets released from the body during exercise. This moisture is in the form of both sensible perspiration (sweat) and insensible perspiration. Insensible perspiration comprises moisture and gasses being released from the body during the normal process of cellular respiration. This means the cells are breathing. The cells are both letting gasses out as well as taking gas in from the environment. This process is needed for detoxification, homeostasis, and feeling good. Synthetic fibers stop or hamper this process.

Body temperature and moisture regulation are closely connected. When moisture can't escape, the body starts struggling to figure out what to do. The whole process of homeostasis—staying at the right temperature—is thrown off. On the one hand, it is cold out there, and warmth is needed. However, overheating is a problem, creating heat stress immediately and later when the sweaty body meets the cold air, turning to cold stress. And at that point, there may be no way to dry oneself when in the backcountry. Staying in synthetic clothing, while at one point may make sense during certain conditions, at other times can be a real problem.

The Actual Mechanism of Moisture-Wicking

Moisture-wicking fabric is a type of textile material designed to draw moisture (such as sweat or moisture from the skin) away from the body's surface to the outer layer of the fabric, where it can evaporate more quickly. This property is achieved through specialized weaving or treatment of the fabric, often with synthetic fibers like polyester or microfiber, which have hydrophobic (water-repelling) properties. Moisture-wicking fabrics are commonly used in sportswear, activewear, and outdoor clothing to help keep the wearer dry and comfortable during physical activities by managing moisture and promoting sweat evaporation, thereby reducing the risk of discomfort, chafing, and overheating.

Polyester and nylon are water resistant because they are made from materials with a particular chemistry that is similar to plastic. Instead of the water being absorbed by the fiber, it sits in droplets on the fiber's surface and moves around the fabric by running along the weave. Eventually, the water droplets reach the outside of the fabric where, if exposed to the air, they evaporate. Because the wicking material does not absorb moisture, the fabric will dry faster.

The dark side of this process is that these fabrics, which wick moisture, also hold moisture next to the skin (think plastic bag). The skin is somewhat suffocating because it is surrounded by plastic…a non-breathable material. The process causes the body to struggle in its moisture and heat regulation efforts.

But the real dilemma is that even though the fabric can wick moisture, it doesn't necessarily make you dry. The ideal situation would be to have a fabric that is both wicking as well as breathable. Breathable fabric lets moisture pass through it. Yes, this seems like a contradiction. How can you let moisture pass through the fabric and have the fabric keep you warm and dry? The fiber that can do this is wool, which will be discussed in the next chapter on natural fibers.

Summary of Problems with Synthetic Fabrics in Clothing, Tents, Sleeping Bags
A Few of the Reasons to Avoid Synthetic Fabrics

- Increases body burden of toxic endocrine disrupting chemicals as skin absorbs endocrine disrupting chemicals.

- Makes you feel clammy because it blocks the release of moisture (sensible and insensible perspiration).

- Contributes to poor body temperature regulation.

- Never can feel as warm as wool due to the clamminess.

- Bocks skin from breathing.

- Stops skin absorbing negative ions.

- Ungrounds body by increasing electric charge on skin. This robs electrons from the body due to the positive charge, decreasing your cellular energy.

- Raises heart rate, preventing deep restorative sleep and relaxation.

- Plastic pollution creates a huge burden on the environment.

Synthetic fabrics, such as polyester, nylon, and acrylic, have significant environmental impacts at various stages of their lifecycle:

- **Fossil Fuel Dependency.** Synthetic fabrics are derived from petrochemicals, meaning they are made from non-renewable resources like oil and natural gas. The extraction, processing, and refining of these fossil fuels are energy-intensive processes that contribute to greenhouse gas emissions, pollution, and habitat destruction.

- **Carbon Footprint.** The production of synthetic fabrics requires substantial energy, resulting in a high carbon footprint. This process emits large amounts of carbon dioxide and other greenhouse gasses, contributing to global warming and climate change.

- **Water Pollution.** During the manufacturing process, synthetic fabrics are often treated with dyes, finishes, and other chemicals. These chemicals can be toxic and, if not managed properly, can contaminate water sources, affecting aquatic life and human health.

- **Microplastic Pollution.** When synthetic fabrics are washed, they release tiny plastic fibers, known as microplastics, into the water. These microplastics are not biodegradable and eventually end up in oceans, rivers, and lakes, where they harm marine life and enter the food chain, potentially affecting human health.

- **Non-Biodegradability.** Synthetic fabrics do not decompose easily. When disposed of in landfills, they can take hundreds of years to break down. During this time, they can leach harmful chemicals into the soil and groundwater.

- **Waste Management.** The difficulty in recycling synthetic fabrics adds to the waste problem. While some synthetic materials can be recycled, the process is often complex and not widely implemented, leading to most synthetic garments ending up in landfills or being incinerated, which releases toxic emissions.

- **Energy Consumption.** Synthetic fabrics require a significant amount of energy to produce, and the ongoing care (like washing and drying) of synthetic clothing also consumes more energy compared to natural fibers, increasing their overall environmental impact.

Natural Fibers

THE STORY OF LINWOOD GORGE

Day 2 Continued...

After a couple of hours of cold, rain, and mist pelting me as I step up and over each rock and slosh through water puddles, I become extremely wet and cold. We stop to get a little shelter under a rock overhang at The Chimneys. My walking stick has been super important as my legs feel weak and wobbly. My fingers have become so numb I am glad I packed my giant homemade butter/cacao bar on the outside pack. I can unwrap it and eat a few bites, drink some water, and when it is time to go, pack up and keep up with everyone else's pace.

I'm so cold I don't really care about anything at this point other than getting to camp and getting into my dry gear. I'm so relieved when the others make a plan for just that. We hike downhill into the gorge, where we will have protection from the wind. When we find the campsite, we each drop our heavy packs and start setting up our tents in the rain. Without any words, we each disappear into our shelters. I don't care about anything at this point, about whether my gear works or not. I can think of nothing other than getting warm. That is the gift of this kind of trip, where you empty your thoughts of everything but the present moment. Every little move is important, and you have no energy to waste on the past or the future.

Most people would call this a miserable day. However, I'm able to get in my tent and sleeping bag and heat some soup during the rain without leaving my tent (tarp). I'm not sure if my gear is working or not. This was as extreme as it gets before I would call it a survival experience. I am so cold it is all I can do to pitch my tarp, throw my gear in, unpack the dry stuff and take off the wet stuff, crawl into my bag and shiver my way back to life.

I eventually warm up as the rain continues to pelt, the wind whips the sides of my tarp, and the temperatures drop. Did my gear completely fail? Well, here I am, recuperating from extremely cold/wet exposure, drying out just as planned inside my amazing wool gear. It seems like it is working pretty darn well. Especially because I can crawl inside my sleeping bag, pull it over my head, and breathe. This creates a heat source not available to campers with synthetic sleeping bags and clothing because if they tried it, they would simply become humid and colder. I won't really know for sure until hours later.

My wool sleeping bag has been doing everything I had hoped it would. So, what is it about wool and other natural fibers that is so helpful? And why didn't I choose down, like goose down, for my sleeping bag when it's commonly used in bedding? Let's take a deeper look at natural fibers.

The first lightweight wool sleeping bag on the market.

An Ex-Marine Transitions to Everything Wool

"I'm an avid camper and spend almost every weekend outside. I transitioned to wool under clothes and found myself so much more happy. Then I bought a wool throw for the house and beach days and have been so impressed. Then, when I'd camp, I'd wake up damp or sticky or whatever in my down bag. I was curious if someone moved forward with a wool bag and found you! Prior to my camping days, I was in the Marines and spent a ton of time outside around the world. The Marines need your bag."
~Testimonial from a Lucky Sheep™ customer

Benefits of Sheep's Wool

- Wool is antimicrobial, dust mite resistant, and hypoallergenic. Excellent for allergy sufferers!

- Wool is a natural insulator, allowing for excellent body temperature regulation.

- Wool fibers allow for moisture to be absorbed and stored as required, keeping the body dry and then released back into the environment.

- Wool offers pressure relief on the body's pressure points when sleeping, leading to less tossing and turning and resulting in a rested night's sleep.

- Wool fibers are difficult to ignite and are self-extinguishing, eliminating the need for fire-resistant treatments.

- Wool is proven to steady the heart rate and allow us to sleep deeper.

Wool Is Truly Moisture-Wicking as Well as Breathable

Not only can wool wick sweat from the wearer, but wool can also move water vapor before it even turns into sweat! Wool is able to release moisture, not just through holes in the fabric, but through the fibers of the fabric itself.

Wool uses a process called "heat of adsorption" to absorb and release moisture. As wool absorbs moisture from the atmosphere, a natural chemical process in the wool releases heat, warming the wearer. In cold weather, the natural crimp in wool fibers creates tiny pockets of trapped warm air that act as insulators, holding in heat next to the body. This same process has a cooling effect in warm weather; as wool releases moisture, it absorbs heat from the wearer, and the tiny pockets of air created by the crimp in the fiber trap cool air and insulate the wearer from warmer outside temperatures. As wool pulls moisture away from your skin to evaporate, you feel cool and dry even in hot weather.

The Superpower of Wool: Heat of Adsorption

Wool has a special ability to manage moisture in a way that makes it ideal for outdoor clothing. Here's what happens:

- **Adsorbing Moisture Releases Heat.** Wool fibers naturally adsorb water vapor from your body or the air. Adsorption means that water molecules get trapped in the naturally porous fibers of the fabric, whereas absorption is where water molecules permeate the fabric and are wet to the touch. For wool, because the water is trapped, it doesn't feel wet to the touch. As this moisture enters the fibers, a small amount of heat is released. This is known as the heat of adsorption, and it is why wool feels warm, even when it's damp.

- **Keeps You Warm in Wet Conditions.** This ability to trap heat while managing moisture makes wool perfect for cold, wet environments. If you're caught in the rain or snow, wool doesn't lose its insulating power the way many other fabrics do.

- **Regulates Your Temperature.** Wool adapts to your body's needs. In cold weather, it traps heat, keeping you warm. In milder conditions, wool pulls moisture away from your skin and helps prevent overheating, creating a balanced and comfortable experience.

This makes wool an all-around excellent choice for outdoor clothing, where moisture and temperature can fluctuate.

How Synthetic Clothing Handles Moisture and Warmth

Synthetic fabrics like polyester, nylon, or polypropylene are engineered to handle moisture in a completely different way. Here's what sets them apart:

- **Repelling Rather Than Absorbing Moisture.** Unlike wool, synthetic fibers don't absorb moisture into their structure. Instead, they are designed to wick sweat away from your skin to the fabric's surface, where it evaporates.

  Synthetic materials, such as pile jackets or synthetic or down-filled sleeping bags sewn with synthetic fabric, do not dry from body heat while wearing. The only way to dry these is in the air or with a fire. This can be a problem during wet conditions where sometimes neither option is available.

- **No Heat from Absorption.** Since synthetic fabrics don't absorb water vapor, they don't release heat when they get damp. If synthetic clothing gets wet (like in a rainstorm), it can often feel cold and uncomfortable because water gets trapped between the fabric and your skin.

With synthetic fabrics the sweat does not leave through the fibers, but rather in between the weave of the fibers. This makes the process of evaporation inefficient because some moisture is always trapped next to the skin.

Wool can be considered an active fiber due to its ability to absorb and desorb moisture vapor as conditions around it change.

Water vapor molecules absorbed by wool attach to specific chemical sites within the structure, losing some of their energy as heat. Thus, moisture absorption by wool as humidity rises increases the fiber temperature, and moisture release following a decrease in humidity lowers it. The amount of heat involved is significant. A kilogram of dry wool placed in an atmosphere of air saturated with moisture releases about the same amount of heat as that given off by an electric blanket running for eight hours. In the Lucky Sheep™ Rewilder20 Wool Sleeping Bag, there are about two pounds of wool batting insulation. This is the equivalent of the amount needed to release heat for eight hours.

Also, inside the wool sleeping bag, the camper can add moisture by breathing inside the bag. That means pulling the top over the head and breathing the warm air inside the bag. The moisture in the breath will be adsorbed into the wool fibers and migrate to the outside, where it will be released. This cannot be done inside a synthetic or down-filled sleeping bag, which would actually make the camper colder by holding the moisture inside but is unique to wool alone.

Wool can be used in base layers as well as insulation layers. Some types of wool even shed water, thus acting as a shell layer.

During a rainy hike, a wool garment will shed the rain (liquid water) but adsorb internally the water vapor generated by the body in response to the effort of hiking. The exact degree to which this works depends on the type of wool fabric. Some wool fabric is made for this type of action.

Key Differences Between Wool and Synthetic Clothing for Outdoor Use

Let's compare wool and synthetic clothing side by side to highlight their advantages and disadvantages in outdoor conditions:

Warmth When Wet

- **Wool.** Stays warm even when damp, thanks to the heat released during moisture absorption.

- **Synthetic.** Loses its insulating ability and can feel cold and clammy when wet.

Moisture Management

- **Wool.** Adsorbs moisture into its fibers, managing it slowly while keeping you comfortable. You can wear wool even when wet, as it will still keep you warm and will slowly dry out from your body heat.

- **Synthetic.** Wicks moisture away from your skin quickly but doesn't retain warmth. Retains some moisture next to the skin.

Drying Time

- Synthetic fabrics such as polypropylene and poly fleece won't actually absorb much water but will be wet and hold the water against you, which will rob you of heat.

- Cotton and other plant materials absorb all the water they can immediately (unless the cotton is treated with wax). Cotton only works as an oilcloth when it is treated with either beeswax, paraffin, linseed oil, or something similar.

- Wool adsorbs a lot of water, slowly and internally; however, the wool still insulates the wearer.

Warmth to Weight Ratio

Many claim wool doesn't work because it has a lower warmth-to-weight ratio than synthetics and down. However, this only applies under ideal conditions. That means dry conditions. And, in effect, this only applies when thought of as static insulation. In reality, where there is exertion, rain, mist, and changing conditions, including wind and exertion level, the synthetic counterparts do not outperform the wool.

Physical exertion, even on a cold day, causes the body to produce warm water vapor. Wool will adsorb the warm vapor, trapping the moisture and the heat inside the fibers. Wool can keep the rain from reaching you while at the same time grabbing the perspiration vapor and heat. When you hike hard in synthetics, the rain will just get you soaked from the inside, even in the clothing that claims to breathe. This is one of the conditions where the wool wins on the warm-to-weight ratio.

Conclusion: Wool's Heat of Adsorption Makes It a Winner for Outdoor Adventures

In 1858, French scientist J. P. Coulier was the first to observe that when dry wool was moved to a humid room where it adsorbed water, it produced heat: the small amounts of energy known as the "heat of sorption." You can notice this in real life when going out on a cold, humid day. Your woolen outerwear will prevent the humidity of the air from chilling you; the wool will dry the air near your body, creating a lower-humidity, warm micro-environment. Wet (high humidity) air pulls heat from the body much more quickly than dry air.

The process of internal adsorption is very gradual and is relatively impervious to liquid water. This is important in cold weather, where heat and energy must be conserved. Physical exertion, even on a cold day, causes the body to produce warm water vapor. Wool will adsorb the warm vapor, trapping the moisture and the heat inside the fibers.

Wool's unique heat of adsorption gives it a significant edge when it comes to outdoor clothing in cold or wet conditions. Its ability to release heat when adsorbing moisture helps you stay warm and comfortable, even in the harshest environments.

Summary of Heat of Adsorption

- Typical wool can adsorb 30 percent of its weight in water without feeling wet because the adsorbed water is trapped inside the fibers.

- The outside of a wool fiber sheds water, so even when wool is literally soaking wet, it will quickly dry off on the outside and feel dry to the touch because the water is only held inside the fiber.

- Wool is also a hygroscopic material. That is, when wool is completely dry, it will adsorb water from the air until it comes to an equilibrium with the surrounding air. This process of equilibration with the surrounding air is called conditioning.

- Inside the wool fiber, water vapor binds to the cortex, producing the heat of adsorption. Again, all adsorption is exothermic: heat generating.

- The body burns a lot of heat to turn liquid water into vapor. Using up excess heat is the reason for perspiration. When perspiration vapor is adsorbed within a wool fiber and then condenses, it slowly releases the heat of condensation: the heat the body expends to create the warm vapor.

- Water molecules are polar, having both a positive and negative side. Once inside the wool fiber, the poles of the water molecules form new bonds with the wool, and the creation of these new bonds releases small amounts of heat: the heat of adsorption.

Scientific Details of the Linen Frequency Study

"In 2003, a study was done by a Jewish doctor, Heidi Yellen, on the frequencies of fabric. According to this study, the human body has a signature frequency of 100, and organic cotton is the same: 100.

The study showed that if the number is lower than 100, it puts a strain on the body. A diseased, nearly dead person has a frequency of about fifteen, and that is where polyester, rayon, and silk register. Non-organic cotton registers a signature frequency of about seventy.

However, if the fabric has a higher frequency, it gives energy to the body. This is where linen comes in as a super-fabric. Its frequency is five thousand."[6]

Wool is also five thousand, but when mixed together with linen, the frequencies cancel each other out and fall to zero. Even wearing a wool sweater on top of a linen outfit in a study collapsed the electrical field. The reason for this could be that the energy field of wool flows from left to right, while that of linen flows in the opposite direction, from right to left.

In an email dated February 10, 2012, Dr. Yellen explained the process of this study:

"Frequency was determined by a technician [named] Ivanne Farr who used a digital instrument designed by a retired Texas A&M professor called the Ag-Environ machine. We had a public demonstration with an audience at internationally known artist Bob Summer's home.

---

6   https://www.academia.edu/39363092/
     Tikkun_Olam_to_Heal_the_World_Wearing_Healing_Flax_Linen_Attire

"Bob Graham, the inventor, told us that his machine was created to analyze the signature frequencies of agricultural commodities to aid the farmer in determining the right time of harvest growth. The gentleman identified signature frequencies that identified illness also and had turned to helping people get well. Bob Graham stated that it was a 'signature frequency of that plant's species identity.' The mHz is different, we were suggested that it would be the same as Rose essential oil.

"Dr. Philip Callahan, a noted physician and researcher, was able to prove the existence of this energy using plant leaves attached to an oscilloscope. About six months ago, he visited me in California and showed me a new development. He had discovered that flax cloth, as suggested in the Books of Moses [the Torah or Pentatuch], acts as an antenna for the energy. He found that when the pure flax cloth was put over a wound or local pain, it greatly accelerated the healing process. He was also using the flax seed cloth as a sophisticated antenna for his oscilloscope. This is the instrument that he uses to determine the energy of flax."

The original source of study is from the original paper linked below: https://www.academia.edu/39363092/Tikkun_Olam_to_Heal_the_World_Wearing_Healing_Flax_Linen_Attire

The Low Down on Down

Down has come to be considered the highest choice for sleeping bags by the majority. Down bags are certainly light and pack really small, but the benefits stop there.

Downfalls of Down

- Down doesn't work if wet, so there is no backup plan in an emergency.

- Down doesn't ventilate, so it cannot regulate body temperature.

- Down can't take humid/damp conditions, so need to zip up inside a tent.

- That tent creates a humid microclimate from insensible perspiration and breathing. This makes you colder.

- Thermal stress causes your body to expend energy rather than restore it.

- Down and synthetic fabric is extremely flammable and needs toxic flame retardants.

- Down is a breeding ground for dust mites.

- Most down is cruelly live-plucked from birds who live in inhumane conditions.

- Toxic chemicals are added to make the down more water-repellant. This actually makes it take longer to dry.

- Down creates "microclimates" where you may be perfectly warm under one section yet roasting in another.

Again, these microclimates cause your body to work hard to keep your body comfortable. Waking up with your head on a sweaty pillow or experiencing that clammy feeling inside the sleeping bag is never enjoyable.

Plus, down is extremely flammable. The only way to reduce this flammability is through potentially harmful chemical saturation of the feathers. As with synthetics, these chemicals can present real problems.

And, of course, in addition to the fire-retardant chemicals, many other chemicals are regularly used in the processing and cleaning of feathers, each with its own possible health risks, especially for people with asthma or any air sensitivities and allergies.

In a controlled study, subjects sleeping in a 64 °F room reported that down tested outside of the comfortable range for optimal sleep.

And, as you learned above, this thermal stress causes you to expend energy rather than restore it.

Down-Filled Sleeping Bags Present Several Environmental Issues:

- **Animal Welfare Concerns.** Down is sourced from birds, primarily ducks and geese. The practices of live-plucking and force-feeding, although illegal in many places, are still a concern. These practices are considered inhumane and cause significant suffering to the animals.

- **Sustainability Issues.** The farming of ducks and geese for down production has an environmental footprint, including land use, water consumption, and feed production. Moreover, conventional farming often involves the use of antibiotics and chemicals that can harm ecosystems.

- **Carbon Footprint.** The processing of down, including cleaning and sterilization, requires significant energy, contributing to the carbon footprint of down-filled products.

- **Chemical Treatments.** Down is often treated with chemicals to make it water-resistant and to prevent it from clumping. These chemicals can be harmful to the environment, especially when they are not disposed of properly.

- **Non-Renewable Resources.** While down is biodegradable, the fabric and materials used in sleeping bags are often made from synthetic, non-renewable resources like nylon or polyester, which contribute to microplastic pollution when they degrade.

- **Waste Management.** Disposing of down-filled sleeping bags can be problematic because they contain both natural (down) and synthetic materials, making them difficult to recycle. Most end up in landfills, where synthetic materials contribute to long-term environmental pollution.

Why Damp Weather Makes Us Feel Colder

Our clothing keeps us warm on cool days by trapping air between our bodies and clothing. The clothing and layer of trapped air prevent our bodies from losing heat by convection currents, which transfer heat by circulating air like a cool breeze on a hot day. Air trapped by clothing cannot easily circulate to transfer heat and cool our bodies. The body must first warm this layer of trapped air to keep us feeling warm.

On a very cool, damp day, however, this layer of trapped air contains water molecules. If it is damp, our clothing is also likely to contain some water molecules. It takes more heat energy to warm water than air. In physics parlance, water has a higher specific heat capacity than air. If the layer of air next to the skin is damp, it, therefore, takes more of the body's heat energy to warm it. Hence, the perceived temperature is cooler.

Why Humidity Makes a Hot Day Feel Hotter

Moisture in the air contributes to your body's cooling processes. It helps to first understand why high humidity on a hot day makes the perceived temperature higher. Sweating is a cooling mechanism. When the humidity is low, sweat evaporates easily. Evaporation requires thermal (heat) energy, so evaporation is a cooling process. When our sweat evaporates, it cools our bodies. On a hot, humid day, sweat does not evaporate as easily, so the body's cooling mechanism does not work as well. The limited evaporation in humid conditions is not enough to cool the body.

When it is cool and humid, the body does not need a cooling mechanism, so the body sweats less. The high humidity does not, therefore, limit evaporation to keep the body warm as it does on a hot, humid day. Additionally, on a cool, dry day, the low humidity does not increase the body's cooling rate as it does on a hot, dry day because most people do not sweat significantly when it is cool.

Therefore, the mechanism that causes humidity to make a hot day feel hotter does not apply in cool weather.

Why Dampness Makes a Cool Day Feel Colder

On a cold rainy day, the falling rain soaks our clothing to make us feel colder. On a cool, damp day, it is less obvious, but our clothing can also absorb some moisture from either the damp air or our bodies. Whether it is raining or simply damp, wet clothing does not keep us as warm as dry clothing for a few reasons.

Even if it is humid, some of the moisture in our clothing can evaporate. Evaporation still serves as a cooling mechanism. This effect is usually small.

The Sleep Environment

We create a warm, humid sleep environment each night by climbing into bed and falling asleep. That's because we generate body heat and perspiration. In fact, we all perspire (and respire) about a cup each night. Just think, your body is 70–80 percent water, and your metabolism is a heat pump. Our bedding is exposed to this heat and moisture. It must manage these conditions efficiently to provide comfortable, restorative sleep.

Due to several synergistic effects, our body temperature, heart rate, and blood pressure rise. As the body's metabolism works throughout the night, perspiration is released as water vapor. Synthetic sleeping bags trap and hold this moisture because air can't circulate. As body heat and moisture build up, your heart rate increases, which elevates blood pressure and causes shallower sleep. A wool sleeping bag promotes air and moisture flow and allows perspiration to evaporate. Thus, the body can cool itself effectively and maintain a comfortable body temperature.

CHAPTER 5

Clothing for Protection from Cold, Wind, and Rain

←———◄◄

THE STORY OF LINVILLE GORGE

Day 2 Continued...

Making Fire in the Rain

After a couple of hours of recuperating from our prolonged cold exposure, we crawl back out of our bags. The rain has stopped. My comrades are scuttling around in the darkness of twilight to get a fire going. How in the world will they make this happen when every stick in sight is drenched? It turns out the leader of this trip has a technique for making a fire starter by putting lint inside a cardboard egg carton and dipping it in wax. It is an amazing tiny fire starter that is virtually bulletproof in the rain. Another guy who has brought a knife carves some slivers of kindling from a fallen limb. It takes some time and coaxing, and there's a big cheer when the little fire finally catches and flares up. The sticks we stacked up in tipi fashion around the fire starter start catching, and then from there, we carefully place more limbs at just the perfect timing across the ever-increasing flame. There is an art to knowing when the fire is strong enough to dry off another limb so the limb can then increase the fire.

Fire has been becoming an essential tool on this backpacking trip; I've come to appreciate it more than I ever had before. There isn't one of us here that successfully saved our clothes. Our experiences are similar in that everything we wore today is in a wet heap in the corner of each of our individual tents. And also, we each saved one bit of clothing and our sleeping bags by having them wrapped in a protective bag and/or pack cover. This answered my question about how my clothing worked compared to theirs. We were all just as wet as the other.

After we each make some dinner, we start drying our clothing articles by holding them near the fire. This isn't always recommended since a flying ember can burn a hole instantly through most fabrics.

Also, it is easy to overheat something by placing it too close to the flame. However, we were willing to take the risk.

I start with my waxed cotton windbreaker and am delighted to find that it dries quickly and is not prone to easily being hurt by the heat or a flying ember. Then I go for socks and a base layer. I can see the steam coming off as the water leaves. It could be considered drudgery; however, the thought of having dry clothes in the morning to start the day propels us on as we each take turns sharing the warm flame, holding clothing articles either in our two hands or sometimes using a stick, and chatting and laughing as the whole prospect of comfort keeps improving.

We retire into our tents for the night. The night is extremely windy; I'm happy we decided to camp down inside the Linville Gorge canyon instead of at the top as originally planned. I put on my base layer, wool socks, and wool sweater and wrap my head in a merino bandana. The extreme wind tests my open tarp, and while I am lying there, I wish I had pitched it lower, but at this point, there is no changing it. All night, the wind whips around, swirling as I listen to the trees creaking and rustling. My tarp is being pushed around a lot, but it does not fail. I pull my sleeping bag over my head and sleep extremely cozy, using my breath as heat. I feel myself dry and thaw out, and I wake up to a surprise—the sunrise is coming up over the mountain, and the skies are blue!

It's a fresh, blue-sky morning; all our clothes are dry and warm, and it's time for breakfast. We've learned about the problems with synthetic and the advantages of natural fibers. As we sit around eating, let's talk about how to go about creating a full set of rewilder's clothing.

My conclusion to the question about how my natural gear measured up to the modern synthetic gear has been answered. My gear worked better overall. We all got wet, we all had a dry change of clothes. However, I was able to use the natural processes of my metabolism in harmony with the elements to remain dry and even become somewhat dryer than I started. If I had crawled into a down sleeping bag, the wetness from my body and clothes would have lessened the warming ability of the sleeping bag. However, in my wool base layer and sleeping bag, I was able to dry out slowly through the night.

Putting the Entire Gear Set Together.

94

Natural fiber outdoor clothing is comfortable, breathable, temperature-regulating, and allows a deeper experience of nature. Natural fibers outperform man-made textiles by allowing a more balanced dynamic between the weather and the body's natural processes of moisture and temperature regulation. I have created a set of outdoor clothing utilizing wool and waxed cotton primarily. This clothing and gear packs into a backpack competitive in weight with the modern gear set for all-year hiking and camping. Each article of clothing coordinates together to create an effective camping experience in all weather/seasons.

A Little History — Natural Fibers Are Old-Timer Approved

As a lifelong outdoor guy, I had gone along with the trends like everyone else, believing synthetics offered better performance and less weight. The buzzword "moisture wicking" was always used to kill any idea that we should use natural fibers. Slowly, my wool sweaters and socks were replaced with pile and polypropylene. There was a period when you couldn't find anything natural in an outdoor gear shop.

I cut my teeth with Paul Petzoldt, who was the Founder of NOLS (National Outdoor Leadership School) and WEA (Wilderness Education Association). He was also an accomplished mountaineer who had an impressive list of major summits to his name including the first attempt at the Himalayan K-2 in 1938. Petzoldt had been doing these things before the advent of synthetic fibers, and he clearly favored wool for many aspects of the outdoor wardrobe. He promoted lambs' wool sweaters as the upper base layer, back before the advent of synthetic outdoor fabrics and before the advent of merino wool base layers. And in pictures of his earlier years, he was wearing wool for both pants and jacket. Paul was all about moisture wicking and ventilation and warned us to stay away from down.

I got to know Paul personally as the youngest of a twenty-two-member, six-week Wilderness Education Association Outdoor Leadership

Training expedition in the Nantahala National Forest, North Carolina. I was a freshman in college, and he was seventy-six years old, teaching one of his last courses before he retired. During this expedition in Nantahala National Forest, he took me under his wing and made sure I had what I needed. He gave me the first pick from a collection of wool sweaters, which were plentiful in that day. Synthetic pile jackets were starting to catch on at the time in 1983. I have always considered this experience a great honor and the roots of my outdoor explorations.

It is Paul Petzoldt who introduced what has become the standards for outdoor leadership training through his schools: the National Outdoor Leadership School (NOLS) and the current Wilderness Education Association (WEA). Looking back on that Outdoor Leadership Training Expedition with Paul Petzoldt, I realize nobody knew the ultimate survival techniques that I would later discover. That course was, for me, the beginning of a lifelong study I would undertake to find the ultimate backpacking gear and, in turn, also discover the secrets of self-healing and longevity.

I learned the industry standard way of doing things from the ground up. Then, over the course of decades, I pioneered new ways of approaching outdoor adventure by applying principles I learned from Ancestral Health. Modern backpacking philosophy comes from a paradigm that is unaware of how metabolism, diet, body mechanics, epigenetics, and biology are involved in outdoor adventures.

The reason this system rocks

- Regulates body temperature.

- Increases exposure to the life-giving negative ions emitted by nature.

- Wicks moisture to the outside.

- Allows that moisture to escape, so you are actually drying things out even during rainy conditions!

96

You can stay warm even in extreme cold conditions or cool during warmer seasons. And if you become over-chilled, you can quickly warm up again from the inside out. You are working with nature to increase your body's ability to adapt to the ever-changing extremes found when we are away from modern structures.

The Synthetic Boom and the Wool Revival

After that experience in 1983, the next few decades would see an explosion of synthetic fibers to the point there was hardly a stitch of wool in an outdoor shop.

Merino Wool Comes on the Scene

In the late 1990s, there was a new resurgence in wool interest spurred on by aggressive marketing campaigns put on by the brands *SmartWool* and *IceBreaker*. Merino wool was the "new kid on the block." Merino is a type of sheep that grows wool that is smooth and silky, not itchy. Merino wool was made into socks, sweaters, and base layers. The amazing fabric called merino wool jersey knit mimicked the look and feel of the popular synthetic stretch tights starting to take hold in the modern wardrobe; it became a popular fabric for tights, leggings, and yoga pants. This merino jersey knit fabric was the best thing for the base layer (which is a fancy way of saying long underwear). The fashion of modern society embraced these stretchy, skintight fabrics, and it became normal to wear them as everyday wear, in addition to hiking and camping clothing.

I was first starting to explore natural fibers for outdoor wear in the year 2010 and it was almost impossible to find even a wool sweater. I scoured the thrift markets and slowly pieced together a few odds and ends of wool sweaters.

Cotton Experiments

Also, there was no longer such a thing as a cotton windbreaker. Everything was synthetic. So I got creative and found some not-perfect-fitting light cotton clothing for pants and a windbreaker. I used a very oversized, five-ounce, tight-weave cotton shirt, which was placed over the wool base layer and insulation layer.

Now, I know cotton is not considered a legitimate fabric for outdoor use. It absorbs moisture like crazy, is worthless when it rains, and can cause hypothermia. However, I was experimenting. It was a starting point of at least finding some way of entering Mother Earth without the shackles of smothering synthetic fibers. And besides, I still had my trusty Gore-Tex so-called breathable jacket. I would later discover how to treat these cotton items with beeswax to create oil-cloth, which repels water.

My Journey of Discovery

I started my outdoor lifestyle in the summer, which was very forgiving. I wanted to see how my body reacted and felt when up against the true test of weather conditions. Besides my wardrobe, I also made my own experimental camping gear, including a backpack, tent, and sleeping bag from natural fibers.

I was nowhere near presentable or fashionable and didn't even tell people what I was doing. I was a "closet camper" just going out to rediscover my place under the sun, hug some trees, write some poetry, and see how far I could take polar plunging in icy waters.

I was thawing out in the sun, getting away from other people's limited belief systems and dogmas about what was the right way to do things outdoors. So much craziness. First, they tell us to wear heavy boots; then they find out we should be going barefoot. It was things like that that had me so confused, and also curious as to what the real truth is. I wanted to discover the true Holy Grail of outdoor clothing.

I have since developed a complete outdoor wardrobe using natural fibers that rocks! I have tested my system in many extreme weather conditions and have gotten it to a point where it excels throughout the year in my region of the Southern Appalachians and is still light and compact enough for backpacking.

From my years of outdoor training, I knew the basics of outdoor dress which I was applying during my creative invention process.

Criteria for Outdoor Clothing

- **Lightweight and compact.** The thickness of the fabric matters. A five-ounce cotton is 50 percent lighter than a pair of jeans, for instance. This also makes a huge difference in volume. Many thin-layered items generally work better than a few thicker items. (This example is only for comparison. Cotton shouldn't be used in most situations unless it is waxed.)

- **Layerable.** The clothing set should be interchangeable and versatile. There should be something for warm weather as well as cold. These can be combined by nesting over each other. For instance, one could have a merino T-shirt and merino shorts in the middle of the day with the sun shining. Then, if the weather changes (rain, wind, cold), one could pull over another layer of merino base layer while still wearing the warm weather set. Consider it the first layer, like underwear. More layers could be added as needed. One could put on an insulation layer (sweater) and/or windbreaker as needed. As you are hiking with a pack, exerting energy, generating heat, and alternating with sitting to rest, you will need different combinations.

- **Movement Friendly (not restrictive).** Tight and restrictive clothing will cut off circulation, causing one to use more energy, feel cooler, and hamper hiking activities. Stretchy merino is ideal for the base layer since it replaces synthetic options such as polypropylene. The shell layers (pants and wind/rain parka) should be loose fitting and allow for the extra layers underneath.

- **Moisture-wicking and breathable.** Anything that holds moisture like a sponge (e.g., untreated cotton) is going to cause misery and be a hypothermia hazard. Similarly, synthetic options that don't breathe can cause overheating and sweating, which later leads to feeling cold. The perfect combination is a base layer of merino wool (this could also be silk), an insulation layer of knitted wool sweaters, and a shell layer of beeswaxed cotton.

- **Eco Friendly.** Considering synthetic fibers are wreaking havoc on wildlife and the environment, this is a good reason to make the switch if you aren't already convinced.

Outdoor Clothing Requires a Three-Step System

1. Base Layer

This is a thin fabric right next to the skin, which is highly stretchable and moisture-wicking. You need a shirt and pants both. It needs to be moisture-wicking because if it traps moisture next to the skin, you will be colder. It needs to be skin-tight because any trapped air will feel cold right next to the skin. It needs to be stretchy because anything constricting will also hamper the body's circulation and heat-generating abilities. Water next to the skin is a big cause of hypothermia. Dry next to the skin creates a feeling of warmth and promotes homeostasis. Because the base layer is so light (it only weighs a few ounces), it is a good idea to bring two sets on a wilderness trek. You may be wearing one during wet weather, and keep a dry set tucked away inside the pack for sleeping.

Characteristics of the Base Layer

- Thin

- Stretchable

- Moisture-wicking

- ➤ Cover both legs and upper body (and head if wintertime)

- ➤ Skin-tight/form-fitting

2. Insulation Layer

In the past, the insulation layer was ubiquitously wool. Then it became replaced with pile (synthetic) jackets and later also with down jackets (down encased inside synthetic fabric). It is not hard to go back to wool. Simple pullover sweaters do the job. One possibility is to use a layering system using two or more sweaters of varying sizes that nest over one another. Just try them on until you get a nice fit. You don't want them to be too tight or too loose. If too tight, they constrict circulation; if too loose, they aren't as efficient (warming). If the outer one pulls on the inner one, you are wasting valuable insulating abilities. So, therefore, get another size up for the outer layer. Layering makes sense so you can adjust for the varying weather conditions. I like 100 percent wool, but if you get an 80 percent wool/nylon blend, it still works.

Characteristics of the Insulation Layer

- Not too constricting

- Not too loose

3. Windbreaker/Wind and Rain Shell/Outer Layer

A wind barrier is extremely critical to survival. Wind chill is a serious factor. No matter how much base layer and insulation layer one has, they will be inadequate in windy conditions. A shell layer comprises both a windbreaker and a rain barrier. It needs to be breathable as well to prevent trapping moisture inside. This layer needs to be carefully fitted over the inside layers so that there is still room to move without constriction. A tight-fitting shell can hamper the heating ability of the system.

Characteristics for the Shell Layer

- Breathable with ways to ventilate when needed

- Wind resistant

- Rain resistant

- Take into account temperature regulation, moisture-wicking, and ventilation.

- Loose fitting, movement-friendly

- Expandable (layers can be added or subtracted underneath)

Windbreaker and Rainshell Outer Layer

Ways to Protect Yourself from the Cold, Wind, and Rain

THE STORY OF LINWOOD GORGE CONTINUED

Day 3

It's day three, and the temps have dropped to about 40 °F, which actually isn't nearly as cold as we expected. You just never know how things are going to turn out on a backpacking trip. We make another fire to sit around while having breakfast, then leave our camp right there and start off on a day hike, which will entail hiking a couple of miles down to the bottom of the Linville Gorge.

It's such a beautiful day. While we hike under the trees and feel the bare ground on our bare feet, let me tell you the story of another hike on a very different kind of day, a day we were caught in a really bad—and unexpected—storm, where I learned some hard lessons about always being properly prepared for any kind of weather event.

The Story of the Big Storm — Learning to Prepare for the Unexpected

In May of 1984, I embarked on an outdoor leadership training expedition with Paul Petzoldt and twenty-one other students in Nantahala National Forest in the Shining Rock Wilderness. which was basically the backyard of the land where I grew up in Cullowhee, North Carolina. During this six-week wilderness trek, we experienced a weather extreme that took us beyond the limits of the gear we had packed. Petzoldt, being the world's most respected outdoor leader at that time, used this opportunity to teach us how to deal with a crisis when in the backcountry. Judgment, discernment, preparedness, emergency plan: all these things were up now as we had to make the most critical decisions of the journey.

We knew we were about to experience a lunar eclipse. There was talk that this could bring extreme weather, and animals would act strangely—whatever that meant. I remember walking away from camp that night to find a place to pee, and the fog was so thick I had trouble walking back to the campfire. What we didn't expect was, that night, after we went to our tents, the wind started picking up. Extreme wind gusts started whipping our tents around. My tent buddy and I spent a mostly sleepless night shivering and wondering if the tent would collapse.

The next day, the storm had blown over to reveal a crystal-clear sky and freezing temperatures. Our water bottles had frozen, and the wind was still strong enough to keep us in our tents, waiting for some signal about what to do next. Some of the other students started coming around, bringing us hot water and telling us how three tents had collapsed and we needed to stay in our tents. Someone had hitched a ride to a nearby town to get some supplies and take an injured student to the emergency room.

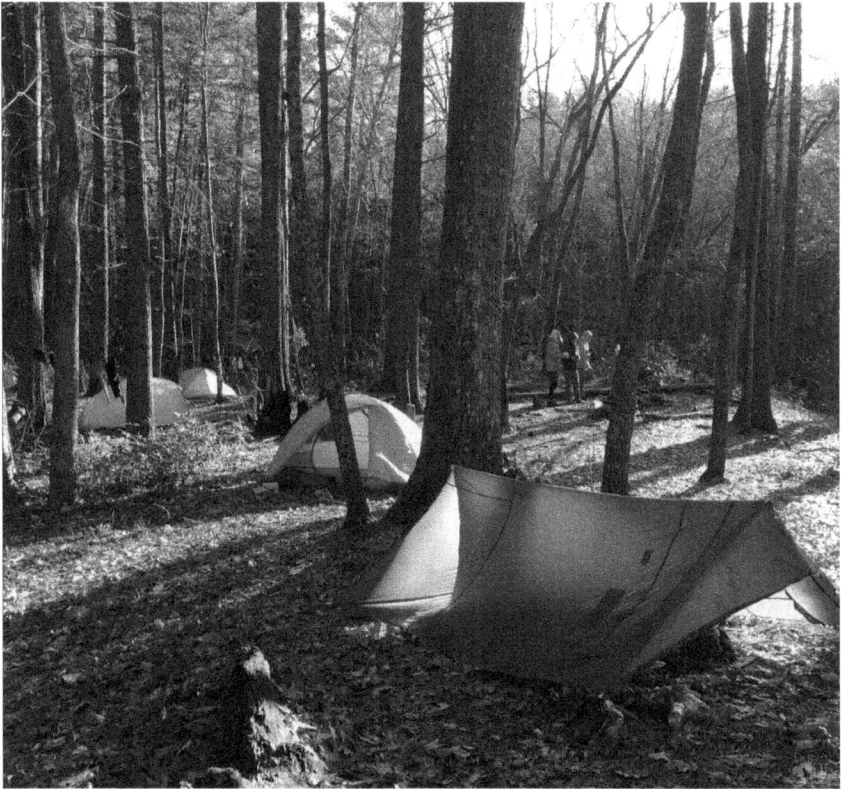

We were caught unprepared. And this was perfect because this is exactly what we need to be prepared for, the unexpected. It was too cold and windy to get out of the sleeping bags because we had packed for spring, and we had a burst of winter. It was so nice to huddle later that day under a south-facing rock overhang out of the wind and get more lessons about how to deal with this kind of situation.

The first thing Petzoldt told us was that he had made a mistake. We were camped in a "wind tunnel" next to Devil's Courthouse (which was a rocky peak in the Shining Rock Wilderness), where we were going to do some rock climbing. In preparation for the storm, we should have moved camp to a place lower down on the ridge. On that cold and blustery sunny day when we couldn't get warm any other way, we gathered at a south-facing rock overhang and talked about the experience and what worked and what didn't. I will never forget how good the sun felt in that cathedral-like rock outcropping, which seemed like the ideal classroom.

←————— ←←

Life Beyond the Trailhead

To be a true Rewilder, you need to get beyond the buildings that comprise the majority of our experience of the world. Then, what you are wearing or carrying in your backpack, well, that's where the buck stops! You can't choose your outdoor gear while considering only one situation. Each condition, in the wild, is multi-faceted and ever-changing. We need to predict the patterns that can happen. And also see the patterns of how the body and the environment interact with weather dynamics.

Synthetic Shell Layers — Problems Resulting from a Lack of Breathability

The shell layer is the outside layer that is meant to shield from rain and wind.

There is a major problem with synthetic shells—lack of breathability. This includes even the so-called "breathable" fabrics such as Gore-Tex. If you have a non-breathable synthetic shell, it works well during certain conditions and not well during others. Another disadvantage of synthetic shell layers is the durable water repellant (DWR) coating wears off, and when this happens, it no longer sheds rain. It is hard to tell when this will happen, and many unwary hikers venture off to find the gear isn't working. This coating needs to be resupplied periodically. The synthetic material is slick and makes a loud swishing noise as you walk, swinging your arms. The synthetic material is easily ripped, so care must be taken when walking through the brush.

Exertion Level Changes

While hiking, you generate heat and sweat. However, when resting, you need more insulation. The gear needs to adapt and work for both high and low levels of exertion, both when the body is generating heat and not generating heat.

Environmental Temperature Changes

A non-breathable synthetic shell might work under below-freezing temperatures or when not exerting much. But in warmer temperatures and exertion, there is a point where you start sweating and overheating. Of course, this can happen even with natural fibers, and the Rewilder will still need to add and subtract layers as described. However, there will be much more breathability with the natural fiber shell.

With a synthetic shell layer, there will be a point of diminishing returns. This means that the so-called technical aspect of the gear—the features that we usually buy the gear for—worked well for a little while but are now not helping and instead are making things worse. At this point, the fact that it is "technical" (concerned with applied sciences) doesn't mean much. The science is still narrow and myopic. Because the gear that was keeping you dry during certain conditions by keeping the rain out is now keeping your body perspiration in, causing your body to overheat and sweat. You can sweat and later become chilled as exertion level and weather conditions change. What is needed at this point is something that is both breathable and wind-resistant.

The Skeleton in the Closet — PFOS in Outdoor Gear

Perfluorooctanesulfonic acid (PFOS) and other forever chemicals (a type of per- and poly-fluoroalkyl substances, or PFAS) are commonly used in outdoor gear for their waterproofing and stain-resistant properties. However, they pose serious health and environmental risks due to their persistence and toxicity. Here's why they're a problem:

Health Risks of PFOS in Outdoor Gear

- **Bioaccumulation in the Body.** PFOS does not break down easily and can accumulate in human tissues over time, leading to long-term health effects.

- **Hormonal Disruption.** PFOS can interfere with the endocrine system, leading to reproductive and developmental issues.

- **Increased Cancer Risk.** Studies link PFOS exposure to an increased risk of kidney, liver, and testicular cancers.

- **Immune System Suppression.** PFOS has been shown to weaken immune function, potentially reducing vaccine effectiveness and increasing susceptibility to infections.

- **Liver and Kidney Damage.** High levels of PFOS exposure have been linked to liver toxicity and kidney disease.

- **Developmental Effects in Children.** PFOS exposure during pregnancy can lead to low birth weight, developmental delays, and learning problems in children.

Environmental Problems of PFOS in Outdoor Gear

- **Persistence in Nature.** PFOS is extremely resistant to degradation, meaning it lingers in soil, water, and air for decades.

- **Water Contamination.** When PFOS-treated gear is washed or discarded, the chemicals leach into waterways, contaminating drinking water supplies.

- **Harm to Wildlife.** PFOS accumulates in the bodies of animals, affecting their reproductive health, immune function, and overall survival.

- **Airborne Pollution.** PFOS can enter the atmosphere through manufacturing processes and eventually settle in remote ecosystems like the Arctic.

- **Bioaccumulation in the Food Chain.** PFOS builds up in fish, birds, and mammals, leading to toxic effects in species higher up the food chain (including humans).

What's Being Done

- **Regulations and Bans.** Many countries have restricted or banned PFOS use, but alternatives like short-chain PFAS may still be harmful.

- **PFAS-Free Outdoor Gear.** Some brands are developing PFC-free waterproof coatings using wax, silicone, or plant-based treatments.

- **Consumer Awareness.** People are demanding non-toxic, eco-friendly outdoor gear, pushing brands to switch to safer materials.

Microplastic Pollution

Microplastics are small fragments that are actively shed from synthetic textiles throughout their lifecycle. A single clothing item in just one laundry cycle has the potential to release as many as 120,000 to 730,000 microfibers, much of which ends up in large bodies of water.

There can be thousands of chemicals added to plastics for several product-enhancing properties. These chemicals are contained in the microplastics and thereby are able to further spread and contaminate the environment and animal as well as population health. A particularly harmful substance present in microplastics is those exhibiting estrogenic properties, which cause severe implications for hormonal wellbeing in animals and especially impact animal fertility and reproductivity.

Microfiber shedding is of cause for serious environmental concern, with the release of primary synthetic fiber fragments from textiles estimated to be 500,000 metric tons annually.

Washing synthetic clothing in laundry machines releases a discharge containing a high number of microplastics into the environment via wastewater. Microplastics can harm wildlife, nature and human health. Once released into the environment, microplastics remain unchanged and are nearly impossible to recover.

Unfortunately, microfiber pollution is not limited to aquatic environments; fiber fragments can also contaminate terrestrial environments such as soil and land, as well as airborne fragment emissions in factories, which can lead to adverse health impacts such as chronic lung disease in workers.

Oil Cloth to the Rescue!

Cotton is not practical to bring on outdoor adventures because you have to plan for wet conditions. It is miserable at best to wear anything cotton when wet as it acts as a sponge and can quickly lead to hypothermia, which is where the slogan "cotton kills" comes from.

This is where oilcloth comes in, which is a tight weave cotton that is treated with beeswax or similar natural oil and wax substance.

Before the advent of synthetics, the shell layer was made from tightly woven light (five-ounce) cotton or silk or a heavier canvas until it became replaced across the board with synthetic. Historically, this cotton or linen was sometimes coated with animal fat, beeswax, or linseed oil and called "oilcloth." This goes as far back as the Vikings and beyond.

I experimented with converting an oversized, lightweight cotton shirt into oilcloth. This actually worked well and this is an inexpensive way for hikers to get a waxed rain layer. Or you can purchase a more technical Bees Waxed Canvas Rain Parka from Lucky Sheep™.

Normally, pants are fairly wind-resistant automatically. However, bulky canvas-type pants like jeans are no good. They restrict movement, and this alone will hurt the body's ability to stay warm. And pants that collect and hold moisture are no good, as anyone will testify who has been caught in them during a rainstorm. This rules out all cotton pants unless they are thin, loose-fitting, and treated with beeswax.

What works even better is wool pants, which are breathable and rain-shedding. These can be made from varying grades of wool, depending on the season and climate. Wool pants feel more comfortable than waxed cotton during rain. Wool comes in several types, which are not itchy, and wearing a merino base layer under more rough wool pants often works very well.

The idea of plastic rain pants doesn't make sense because the legs sweat more than the torso. So, any attempt to keep the rain off like that when hiking is also going to cause overheating and sweating.

Some people use plastic skirts or kilts as well as ponchos, which allow more ventilation. Again, this works in some situations but it is still a compromise with breathability.

Problem: synthetic fibers have limitations for the shell layer due to lack of breathability.

One solution that has worked is waxed cotton or oilcloth used for the upper shell and pants. Alternatively there are also some types of wool jackets and pants which work as well. It is a matter of trying things out to find which solution best suits your needs. One will need to tailor their choice of gear for the type of adventure and according to which season it is.

Carrying the Burden

Lightweight backpacking refers to a style of backpacking where the base weight of the pack is minimized to enhance comfort and efficiency while still maintaining safety. In recent years, with the development of new NASA-developed synthetic fabrics and chemicals for treating down, there has been an obsession with reducing the weight of the pack beyond anything previously possible. In our attempts to get closer to Mother Nature, we often end up wrapping ourselves in several layers of plastic along with the many hazardous chemicals that come with them. Some people give up on these ultra-light levels due to compromises in comfort and safety.

Weight Classifications in Backpacking

- **Traditional Backpacking.** Base weight of 30+ lbs. (13.6+ kg).

- **Lightweight Backpacking.** Base weight of under 20 lbs. (9.1 kg).

- **Ultralight Backpacking.** Base weight of under 10 lbs. (4.5 kg).

- **Super Ultralight Backpacking.** Base weight of under 5 lbs. (2.3 kg).

Key Terms

- **Base Weight.** The total weight of your backpack, excluding consumables (food, water, and fuel).

- **Consumable Weight.** The weight of food, water, and fuel which varies depending on trip length and conditions.

- **Total Pack Weight.** The combined weight of base weight and consumables at the start of a trip.

There is good reason to scrutinize weight and make sure every little thing is necessary and designed well. Each ounce we carry causes us to burn more calories. There are only so many calories we can burn before we are worn out—or done hiking for the day. This is what has driven the backpacking market toward these high-tech, lightweight synthetics. When we focus only on the weight-to-warmth ratio as the only factor in choosing gear, we are leaving out the rest of the qualifications for good gear, such as effectiveness at dealing with adverse conditions, comfort, sleep quality, and environmental stewardship. Essentially, adding three pounds of weight to the pack, at the end of the day, will cost you about three-quarters of a mile on a twenty-mile trek.

Pack weight lbs.	Pack weight kgs	Calories burned per hour	Speed (Miles per hour)	Miles per day	Kilometers per day	Calories burned per day
15	6.80	451.25	2.6	20.8	33.47	3610
17	7.71	460.75	2.56	20.48	32.95	3686
20	9.07	475.00	2.5	20	32.18	3800
25	11.33	498.75	2.4	19.2	30.89	3990
30	13.6	522.5	2.3	18.4	29.61	4180
35	15.87	546.25	2.2	17.6	28.32	4370
40	18.14	570	2.1	16.8	27.03	4560

What to Do in Different Weather Conditions

Allowing Yourself to Get Wet in the Rain

During the summer months, I started wondering if letting myself get wet sometimes would be the best option. The thing that drove this home was when I was hiking in a pouring thunderstorm in the summer and wearing my last item of synthetics, which was a so-called "breathable" Gore-Tex parka over a merino base layer. I was overheating and feeling like I should just take the parka off and get wet. I finally did that, and I was cold and wet (from the rain) but felt better than being hot and wet (from sweat).

This changed my approach. It is not black and white. We don't only need protection from the rain, but we also need to maintain homeostasis in the body. That means temperature regulation, and that means moisture wicking, breathability and ventilation.

So, I started trying out some new techniques. In summer, I started sometimes wearing a merino top and bottom and just getting wet. That evolved into wearing wool shorts and minimalist sandals for the bottom, letting the waist-down part get wet. For the top, I could wear a synthetic poncho with a wool felt rain hat or umbrella. And finally, I replaced my synthetic poncho with my own beeswaxed canvas rain parka. The problem with ponchos is they can get in the way of walking because they obstruct the ground beneath. Another disadvantage of the poncho is that it is not very protective in windy conditions.

There are many conditions that call for various approaches to ventilation versus tightening up every wind hole. Let's look at certain examples one might encounter on a backpacking trip or day hike, along with an appropriate gear approach:

Below Freezing and Windy

Wear the shell/parka completely cinched up so no air gets through at the waist, wrists, or neck/face. If you overheat, start uncinching the openings so a little air gets in. If that's not enough, take the parka

114

off and either hold it in case you need to put it back on, put it in or attach it to your backpack, or drape it over your head so it offers a little protection but allows maximum ventilation.

I have personally hiked in extremely windy and cold situations (wind chills approaching -20 °F) where the wind shell was too hot because I was climbing quickly and with a lot of exertion. I might start out with my Waxed Canvas Shell; then, I would need to take it off as I warmed up. During the heavy climbing, I would be too hot and start to sweat with it on. What I was wearing under the shell was my simple merino base-layer shirt. I would put the parka back on if I needed to stop for a break. Sometimes, I would have two layers of the merino base layer shirt.

Waist down, I had lightweight beeswaxed cotton pants with a merino base layer underneath.

Also, I had wool socks, minimalist boots, wool mittens, and merino wool headwraps.

In these situations, one needs to be in touch with their body, go slow and check in with oneself to see if any adjustments need to be made. Frostbite and hypothermia can set in fast, especially in windy conditions.

Below Freezing and Snowing

With snow, more protection from getting wet may be necessary. Wearing a broad-brimmed wool felted hat is one of the best things. Also, it is more likely you will need to keep the parka on or at least use it draped over yourself while open. It can also be draped over the backpack.

33–45 °F and Light Rain

These conditions would call for a similar approach to the one above. You would simply be removing the parka more often, wearing it draped and open over you.

33–45 °F and Heavy Rain

You might possibly consider an umbrella in heavy rain, along with draping the parka over you and opening it. If it was also windy, the umbrella may not work. Then you would use your parka hood and possibly a wide-brimmed felted wool hat over it.

45 °F and Above with Light or Heavy Rain

With light rain, the parka draping technique is great. Sometimes, even this can be too hot. Sometimes, just getting wet is the best option to prevent overheating. It depends a lot on the individual. The umbrella comes in the best during warm, wet conditions, when wearing anything can overheat, and yet you don't want to get drenched. Oftentimes, exposing yourself to some light rain doesn't get you any wetter than sweating, even on a dry day. And the cool rain can sometimes feel welcoming. Remember, the merino base layer wicks moisture and keeps you feeling somewhat dry even when it gets wet.

Bonus Tips: Make a Simple Oil Cloth Windbreaker from an Oversized Cotton Shirt

You might want to alter the shirt by removing the buttons and adding a zipper. Also, put a hood at the top and large hand pockets at the bottom. Otherwise, this idea will only work marginally at best.

Place one pound of beeswax, four ounces of linseed oil, and one-quarter-cup pine resin in a metal or ceramic bowl and then inside a crock pot. Alternatively, place it in a larger pot with a couple of inches of water on the stovetop.

Set heat on low and let ingredients melt. Stir occasionally.

Turn off and pour into muffin tins. Let it cool down. It will solidify into the mold of the muffin tins. Place in a cool place until it solidifies. Take it out, turn it upside down on a cutting board, and give it a tap or two until it falls out. If it's having trouble coming out, place it in the freezer for a few minutes or longer and then try.

Rub one of these bars onto the fabric until the surface is coated thoroughly.

Place the shirt on cardboard and use an iron to melt the wax. You may want to use wax paper between the iron and the cloth to keep the iron from accumulating wax. The wax is going to melt through and seep into whatever is on the other side. So make sure you are safe. Then iron in. Then, do another section. Keep going until the entire shirt is coated.

You will also want to put a layer on the surface which doesn't get ironed in. Instead, use a blow dryer to set it. This surface coating is important to create a complete water seal.

If you find you've missed places (inevitable) you can easily re-coat and re-iron any time.

The iron will get some wax on it, but clean it by simply rubbing it on a scrap cloth when you are finished before the iron cools down.

You can also use this method on cotton pants as well as other gear such as tarps and backpacks.

You can also purchase these bars already made at Lucky Sheep™.

CHAPTER 6

Rewilding Your Feet

THE STORY OF LINWOOD GORGE

Day 3 Continued...

I have never eaten so well on a backpacking trip. My new Paleo recipes are delicious and provide vital warmth and energy. Our trip leader had been making it super easy by boiling a big pot of water that we each could pour over whatever food or beverage we brought along. I explained to my new friends what I was eating, and they could barely comprehend. I was having blueberry pemmican, which is an ancient Native American recipe. You combine meat and berries, pulverize them, and mix that with rendered lard (animal fat) to make a nutrient-dense, mouth-watering, life-giving food. Plus, you just pull it out and start eating. Since this is prepared at home, there is no cooking involved at camp. It only takes a few bites to be completely satisfied and ready to hit the trail. Add to that a cup of coffee or tea and generous chunks of butter, and you have a powerhouse trail breakfast. This pemmican can also be combined with boiling water and vegetables or herbs to create a satisfying warm stew.

We decide to take a leisurely packless day hike down the trail to visit the Linville River at the bottom of the Gorge. We hang our remaining wet clothing articles on lines strung between trees to dry before we hike. At this point, I don't think any of us are trying to set any records but mostly just wanted an enjoyable experience. Putting one's body up against nature in its extremes has a way of humbling a person. I took off my shoes and shirt and hiked pack-free while enjoying the morning sun on my skin.

The day was the lowest and then the highest elevations of our hikes as we went down to the wild Linville River and then back to camp to pack up and hike with packs up to the highest point of Table Rock Mountain. From there, we hiked on the Mountains-to-Sea Trail to a camp in the Wilson Creek Wilderness.

Feet Rewilding

And what was I wearing on my feet for all this hiking? How do we rewild our shoes and feet to be as close to our ancestor's ways and to be most attuned to the earth?

The old-school philosophy is to wear waterproof and heavily protective boots for hiking and backpacking. Evidence from the Ancestral Health movement is showing us that our modern shoes are weakening our feet, misaligning our toes, interrupting the entire structure (posture) of the body, and hurting our balance. When we wear modern, thick-soled shoes, our feet do not function as they are designed. When we go barefoot, we start to realize our full potential with strength and flexibility. The common paradigm of overprotectiveness and over-padded has led to the degeneration of our feet.

Why Hike in Barefoot Minimalist Shoes?

Most modern hikers will tell you that you need a waterproof boot with a hard shell and ankle support to be equipped correctly for long hikes, although this has been increasingly replaced with lighter boots and sneakers. Even these miss the point, which is to get rid of the foot support and over-padding of the rubber soles. And while I agree that those qualities can be helpful in certain situations, there is an argument to be made for wearing a shoe that allows you to feel the earth mimicking something closer to barefoot walking.

Minimalist shoes are lighter and more comfortable than hiking boots. The reason, of course, is that hiking boots are made to protect you. If a rock lands on your foot or you twist your ankle, hiking boots have a much better chance of keeping you injury-free.

However, sturdy, hard-soled, heeled hiking boots or even sneakers that have arch support and tipped forward angles weaken our feet and ankles and throw the entire body and gait out of alignment.

There is one very important thing to know. Do not simply throw away your standard footwear. Minimalist shoes should only be used when the hiker has thoroughly developed a Rewilder's feet and body.

To those who want a near-barefoot, quiet experience when they hike, minimalist shoes or boots are a great option. Alternatively, one could bring moccasins or minimalist shoes and wear them part-time around camp and on day hikes as part of the training process. Those who just want a pleasant camp shoe might also give it a try.

There is a process to adopting a barefoot lifestyle. Generally, it involves going barefoot and barefoot shoe wearing in short increments, along with daily massaging of the feet with some kind of roller. You can do this even while standing to work on a computer or watching a video. You build up to more time spent barefoot as part of the total body rewilding process.

Features of Rewilding Shoes:

- Very thin and flexible sole (minimalist), low to the ground for balance and agility.

- No arch support.

- No heel (zero drop).

- Wide toe area so the toes can spread out.

- Ideally, the fabric would be either canvas or leather for the same reasons it's good for the clothing to be non-synthetic—to allow the feet to breathe.

- Drain holes for shedding water. The idea is to let the feet get wet and drain at the same time. Wearing wool or alpaca socks is the key to making this system work. This means you want to avoid boots with a Gore-Tex-like waterproof liner. You want the opposite, a shoe that allows air and moisture to move in and out easily.

- Some amount of tread is necessary to keep from slipping in rugged and sometimes muddy or icy terrain. However, Native Americans wore moccasins without tread, so it is possible but extreme. You also should bring some type of crampon clip-on device to wear during icy conditions.

There are several companies with minimalist boots/shoes specialized for trail hiking, such as *VivoBarefoot*, *Softstar*, *Xero Shoe*, and *Earth Runners*. Some terrains allow for the safe use of sandals. This is ideal when on more flat, dry trails, not ones that are muddy and without a lot of roots and edges to snag and stub toes.

For a complete education on movement therapy and action plan on rewilding your feet and body check out Katy Bowman's books and classes at nutritiousmovement.com

CHAPTER 7

Putting Your Entire Gear Set Together

←————◂◂

THE STORY OF LINWOOD GORGE CONTINUED

Day 3 Continued...

Again, more fires and more testing of my tarp and natural fiber gear; however, this time, without rain.

It's a delight to camp near a creek, which we approached in the dark and pitched camp and made fire again in the dark.

I am extremely pleased with my open-air tarp and natural fiber moisture-wicking gear. Camping near a creek can feel cold in the winter because of the dampness. And this is just what I love because where before the gear worked counter to the circumstances, here my wool setup is ideal. I feel warm and dry. The others are going in their tents trying to protect their down from absorbing moisture, which would weaken its thermal abilities. And this is impossible to do because when we try to keep the outside moisture away, we then close the tent up to keep the body moisture inside (from breathing).

It's the morning of the fourth day. It's a sunny day, and I slept amazingly. My friends almost had to wake me up since I was still asleep after they were done with breakfast and packing to leave.

THE END OF THE STORY OF LINWOOD GORGE

In the above story, my gear kit adapted to the circumstances and supported me in numerous ways over the four-day backpacking trip. This was even before I had developed it further with the current beeswaxed rain parka and improvements on the waxed canvas backpack.

We each need to develop a relationship with our entire gear set and know how to alternate different articles of clothing with varying conditions. And the best way to do this is to test each item near home on walks in the park as well as day hikes during varying weather conditions.

We Were Testing the Gear on Five Tests. How Did It Do?

Answer:

1. Overall pack weight. My gear gets a four out of five. It was a bit heavier, but not unreasonably.

2. Overall functionality of gear when faced with weather extremes such as rain, cold, wind, etc. My gear gets a four out of five. We all got drenched to the bone. My gear was able to dry out even in these extreme conditions. Others complained about never feeling warm on the trip. My reasoning is that they were experiencing the clammy effect of synthetic fabric, clothing, and tents, which traps moisture next to the skin. I later added wool pants to my gear instead of waxed cotton, and this performed even better.

3. Carrying not too much and not too little of anything (such as water, food, etc.). My gear gets a five out of five. I had a little

126

extra food at the end, which is just the right amount because you always want to carry extra. I used every article of clothing at one point or another and needed it all. That means I carried enough and not too much. I used everything I brought.

4. Overall comfort and enjoyment of the experience. (For instance, even if a pack is light, is the person still warm and well-fed and able to adjust to the changing conditions found in nature?) My gear gets a four out of five. I was able to dry out when necessary and hike with relative comfort through varying conditions. I also slept very well. I will need to bring my own fire equipment if this is not provided by the group. That would include a small hatchet, matches, and beeswax fire starters.

5. Having everything you need. (This means not leaving an important item out and being prepared for emergencies such as first aid and survival items.) My gear gets a three out of five. I didn't carry some of the extra gear that others had, such as a saw, ax, and emergency items. If I had, my pack would have been heavier. If I had gone alone, I would have needed to carry these items. This is something I need to improve on and get some extra gear, such as a lightweight ax or saw and fire starter. I also need to learn more about starting fires in the rain.

Summary

Here are the basic building blocks of the natural outdoor gear system:

- **Wool, which heats the body as it dries out.** Solves: getting chilled when wet. Some of the best night sky viewing is in open meadows and prairie. However, these are the places you are likely to encounter dew. Just beware, as this can lead to a bad night as you struggle to adjust to the changing conditions, which ultimately might leave you drenched and cold. The remedy to this is to use wool bedding instead of cotton, down, or synthetic. I spent decades struggling with this until I discovered wool. There is nothing else as powerful for wicking moisture and keeping you dry. Even if the outside is drenched, the inside stays perfectly dry. With wool, you can wake up with no idea the area is covered in dense fog or dew until you get out of your sleeping bag.

- **A Bees-Waxed Canvas Rain/Wind Shell.** Solves grounding to the body and allows better temperature regulation. Also does not burn from a spark coming out of the fire, nor tear when walking through brambles.

- **A Tent or Tarp Which Is Not Sealed at the Bottom and Open on Each End.** Solves condensation and cold due to moisture. In good weather, the open sky is the ultimate. But if you do this, you want to have a tent set up nearby in case it does rain. The best all-round alternative is a tarp, which allows fresh air but protects from the rain. There is an amazingly simple tarp system available, which can be set up in five minutes anywhere, only weighs about two pounds, and fits two people including gear.

- **Trekking Poles or Two 3-Foot-Long Sticks of Wood Found Almost Anywhere.** You will also need a ground cloth under this as well as a closed-cell insulated foam sleeping pad.

- **A Wool Felt Hat and/or Umbrella Which Allows Ventilation.** Solves trapping moisture and also prevents some glare without using sunglasses.

- **Minimalist Shoes Which Allow Proper Alignment of the Body While Walking and Build the Feet's Muscles Instead of Atrophying Them.** They also prevent blisters and foot cramps. However, one needs to adapt to minimalist shoes before hitting the trail. Solves body posture and foot muscle development and prevents blisters and foot cramps. Feet also stay warmer when wearing a properly fitting pair of minimalist shoes/boots because the feet are moving more which aids better circulation.

Principles and Reasoning

- **Wool Felt Hat and Waxed Jacket.** This allows air circulation similar to an umbrella. (Other options are a poncho or an umbrella.) You don't absolutely need the felt hat if the parka has its own hood. The brimmed hat, however, makes it easier to see around you as you are walking than a hood. The hat is also used to cut the sun's glare during bright days.

  - **Let Yourself Get Wet from the Waist Down.** In summer, this applies to shorts, which should be wool. In colder weather, wool pants can get wet and still keep you warm without overheating. If you try to make your boots waterproof (with waterproof liner, etc.), that keeps the water in, so your feet don't dry out. So, a leather minimalist shoe that is treated with beeswax is ideal.

  - **Keep a Set of Clothes Tucked Away in a Waterproof Bag** reserved for wearing at camp only. Include a merino top and bottom, wool socks, hat, and sweater. This is one place where I use synthetic, in the form of a silnylon or drawstring bag inner liner.

  - **The Tent/Tarp Needs to Allow for Excellent Ventilation.** A zip-up close-able tent can trap moisture/humidity and stifle the temperature regulation process, just like a synthetic parka. The Ray-Way tarp idea (a simple tarp with open sides) solves the problem and makes a more fun, interactive camping experience. This also includes a net tent that goes inside when there are insects.

◆ Clothing and Sleeping Bag Should Be Wool.
The reason is to provide superior moisture wicking, ventilation and temperature regulation.

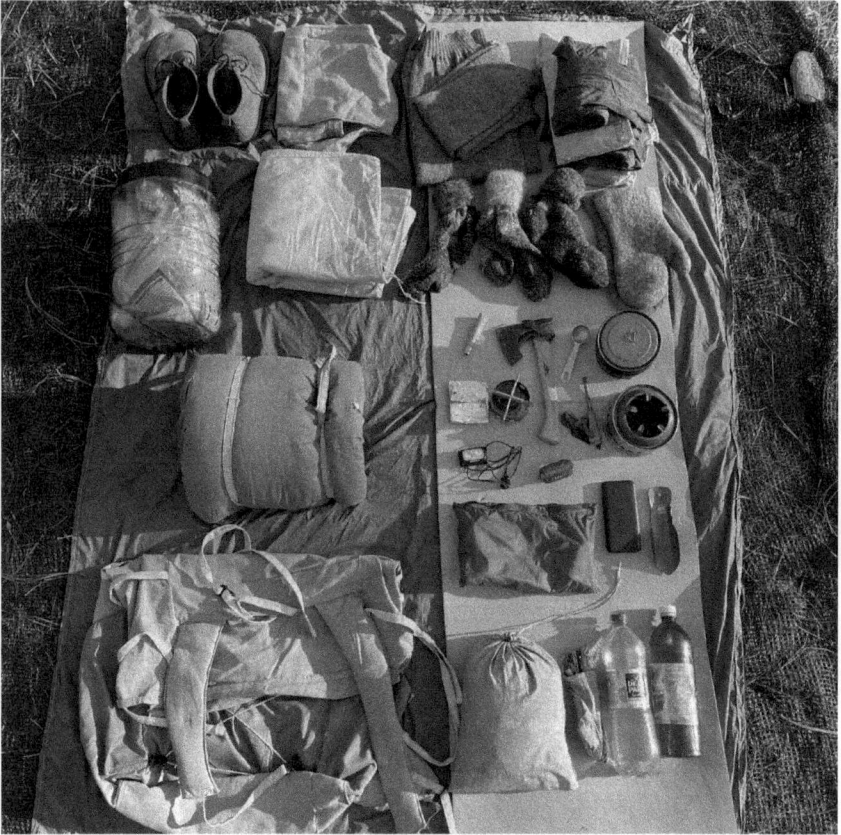

Barefoot minimalist boots, wool pants, alpaca sweater, wool base layers tops and bottoms (2 each), Food (in bear canister), beeswax canvas rain parka, alpaca socks (3pr.), wool mittens, wool sleeping bag, pocket knife, hatchet, titanium cook pot, twig stove, flint fire starter, alcohol burning stove, flashlight, blinking red light, first aid/toiletries kit, battery pack, trowel, beeswaxed canvas backpack, silnylon tarp and bug tent, tent stakes, water bottles.

Rewilder's Backpacking Checklist
Type of Trip: A multi-day backpacking expedition
Temperatures: Temperatures from 20–80 °F
My Gear Includes:

Base Layer

- Merino wool top and bottom (two to three sets). This includes one short-sleeved merino t-shirt and one pair of merino shorts for warmer months. This first layer is similar to underwear, but I also wear it as an outer layer on a hot day. This way, I can layer one, two, or three as needed. Jersey fabric is the same kind of stretch material we are all accustomed to with T-shirts. However, when this jersey cloth is made from merino wool, you get a silky soft effect with the ultimate stretchability. It feels warm to the touch but also can feel cool on a humid, hot day.

- Merino bandana and merino headwraps (two). These headwraps are like hats but with no top. They can be placed around the head and ears, or around the face, or around the neck (one in summer, two or more in winter). They can be layered as many times as needed to create a thicker/warmer effect.

Insulation Layer

- Wool sweaters (one, two, or three depending on season, which nest over each other).

- Wool socks. Three pairs (one for only sleeping, one for wearing, one for washing).

- Wool finger mitts, wool mittens, or wear wool socks over the hands.

Shell Layer

- Waxed cotton parka or poncho (for warmer months).

- Wool pants or waxed lightweight cotton pants.

- Wide-brimmed felted wool hat.

Other

- Wool shorts (or waxed lightweight cotton).

- Shoes (one pair of minimalist boots, and in summer, one pair of minimalist sandals, optional).

- Wool mittens, finger gloves, hats, and scarves as needed, depending on season/climate.

- Crampons (a metal traction device that is fixed to footwear to improve mobility on snow and ice).

Shelter Items

- Tarp tent

- Net tent

- Closed-cell foam sleeping pad

- Silnylon ground sheet

Food Items

- Cooking kit

- Water bottles (2-liter soda bottles work great!)

- Stove with fuel

- Bowl

- Spoon

- Bear hanging bag or bear canister

- Food (more on this in the Food chapter)

- Fire-making tools (hatchet, knife, matches, etc.)

Twig gasifier stove, flint fire starter, titanium pot.

Other Items

- Flashlight

- Ziplock bags

- First aid kit

- Electronics

- Maps/compass

- Writing and reading materials (optional)

Complete Rewilding
Backpacking Gear Checklist

CLOTHING

SHELL LAYER

Shell Jacket—Cotton/beeswax oilcloth . . . . 30 ounces

This replaces the synthetic Goretex style modern shell

https://www.woolsleepingbag.com/product/beeswaxed-rain-parka/

Pants-Wool

Can be worn in rain, let them get wet. Still insulating.

winter weights: www.weatherwool.com

summer lighter weight: www.lucky-sheep.com

Umbrella . . . . 21 ounces

Optional....but comes in handy during certain conditions, especially warm rainy or extreme sun.

www.zpacks.com

INSULATION LAYER

Wool Sweaters. . . . . .16-32 ounces

(nesting sizes thickness depending on season) finer wools such as lamb's wool, Cashmere, alpaca, or merino are the warmest and lightest

Often found at thrift stores for very cheap, or buy new online.

BASE LAYER

Merino Long Sleeve Top. . . . . 6 ounces

In winter, bring two each, one to wear while hiking and one for sleeping or to double up

https://danishwool.com/products/copy-of-hocosa-sport-organic-merino-wool-long-sleeve-undershirt-for-men-or-women-round-neck-in-black-or-red

Merino Leggings. . . . . 6 ounces
In winter, bring two each, one to wear while hiking and one for sleeping or to double up

https://danishwool.com/products/hocosa-sport-organic-wool-long-underwear-pants-for-men-or-women?pr_prod_strat=jac&pr_rec_id=8cf6a56a6&pr_rec_pid=8067784769842&pr_ref_pid=8110843724082&pr_seq=uniform

Wool Shorts . . . . 2 ounces
Used for hiking in dry or wet weather and for swimming.. . . . .

Merino T-Shirt. . . . . 4 ounces
Can serve as extra base layer and good for warm weather

https://danishwool.com/products/hocosa-short-sleeve-sport-undershirt-in-100-organic-wool-unisex

Merino Underwear . . . . 2 ounces
https://danishwool.com/products/hocosa-womens-organic-wool-1-4-length-wool-underwear-pants?_pos=10&_sid=3463a0b18&_ss=r

FEET

Wool Socks (3 Pairs). . . . . 6 ounes each = 18 ounces
One pair for wearing, one pair for washing, one pair for sleeping only

https://www.etsy.com/listing/494220385/alpaca-socks-all-season-socks-hiking-and?ref=shop_home_feat_1&bes=1&sts=1&logging_key=a4b8d9ebfc0b6a19ee4e05f01fbe374cfc7ee1a9%3A494220385

Minimalist Boots (leather with no liner). . . . . .8-16 ounces
https://www.softstarshoes.com/adult-hawthorne-chukka.html

Minimalist Sandals (optional, for warmer seasons). . . . . . 9 ounces
https://www.earthrunners.com/

HEAD

Merino Bandana / Head Wrap . . . . 2 ounces

https://www.woolsleepingbag.com/product/merino-bandana/

Wool Hat. . . . . 6 ounces

Merino Scarf . . . . 6 ounces

https://www.woolsleepingbag.com/product/merino-wool-scarf/

Wool Felt Crushable Hats. . . . . 6 ounces

This is great for sun as well as rain. Shading the eyes is better than sunglasses when possible.

https://www.overland.com/products/overland-crushable-wool-felt-fedora-hat-67414

FOOD ITEMS

Titanium Pot. . . . . 4 ounces

This is the lightest and strongest metal.

https://zpacks.com/collections/ultralight-pots-mugs-for-hiking

Drinking Mug and Spoon. . . . . 4 ounces

Stove . . . . Alcohol Burning - 4 ounces

I use an alcohol burning stove for more convenience and when there are fire bans.

https://backpackingadventuregear.com/shop/ols/products/etowah-ii-stove-kit

Stove . . . . Twig Gasifier Stove -12 ounces

I use a twig burning stove when I can. The extra weight is balanced out by the fact you don't need to carry fuel.

https://www.silverfire.us/economy-scout-stove.

Lighter / Matches / or Ferro Rod . . . . 1 ounce

https://www.silverfire.us/fire-starters

Alcohol Fuel (for use in alcohol stove) . . . . .4-12 ounces

Get denatured alcohol at your local hardware store or building supply.

Scrubby / Washcloth . . . . 1 ounce

A small cotton rag used to clean dishes comes in handy. It will need a ziplock bag for carrying.

Bear Bag and Cording. . . . . 4 ounces

A bear bag is a stuff sack to put the food in and hang in a tree using proper chording. You also need about 30 feet of strong chord. Alternatively use a bear canister.

zpacks.com

Bear Cannister (optional) . . . . 16 ounces

This is required in some locations and is used instead of hanging a bear bag.

Ziplock Bags for carrying some food items

GENERAL

Flashlight . . . . 4 ounces

Make sure it has a red setting. It's good to have an extra as a backup.

https://zpacks.com/products/nitecore-nu25-400l-headlamp-w-ul-headband

Maps . . . . 4 ounces

In ziplock bag

Small Knife . . . . .2-4 ounces

My favorite is a wooden handled Opinel

Small Hand Hatchet (optional). . . . . 14 ounces

This very light hatchet comes in handy when you want to make fires. Use to cut and split wood.

https://www.gransforsbruk.com/en/product/gransfors-small-hatchet/

Water Filter or Lugols Solution . . . . 2 ounces
Depending on the level of water purity, add 2 drops to 8 drops per liter and wait 20 minutes.

Notepad/Pen . . . . 2 ounces
In ziplock bag

First Aid Kit . . . . 16 ounces

Trowel . . . . 4 ounces
Lightweight digging tool for cat holes . . . .

T.P.. . . . . 4 ounces
In ziplock bag, enough for the days on the trail. . . . .

Baking Soda . . . . 4 ounces
In small plastic bottle. Use it for washing hands and brushing teeth. . . . .

Toothbrush . . . . 2 ounces

Cell phone device (optional) or other electronics, solar charger, battery pack, etc. . . . . .8 ounces - 16 ounces
Also used for navigating with Topo Apps. . . . .

SHELTER

Tarp / Tent . . . . 16 ounces
Silnylon works well and open on both ends. If bugs are an issue also use a net tent inside.
https://www.rayjardine.com/ray-way/Tarp-Kit/index.php

Stakes . . . . 8 ounces

Ground Cloth . . . . 4 ounces

Net tent (optional depending on conditions) . . . . 8 ounces
https://www.rayjardine.com/ray-way/Tarp-Kit/index.php

Sleeping Pad . . . . 16 ounces
Closed cell foam is my first choice for durability and effectiveness against the cold.
https://www.campmor.com/products/
therm-a-rest-ridgerest-closed-cell-foam-pad-regular

Sleeping Bag . . . . 4 lbs. (64 ounces)
Lucky Sheep™ Rewilder Lightweight Wool Sleeping Bag.
https://www.woolsleepingbag.com/product/wool-sleeping-bag-lightweight/

Trekking Poles (optional) . . . . 16 ounces
These are not in the pack most of the time, you can also use walking sticks you find on the trail, or make your own at home if you like wood carving.

BACKPACK

Backpack . . . . 21 ounces
This should be in the range of 40–70 Liters carrying capacity.
https://www.woolsleepingbag.com/product/canvas-backpack-organic-non-toxic/

PART 3

Food

CHAPTER 8

How We Eat Our Environment

The food we eat matters because native food syncs our brain and body to our native habitat. The closer it is to our pre-industrialized ancestors, the better. In temperate climates, that means a focus on saturated fat and red meat grown on organic pastures with mineral-rich soil along with some starches.

Food, Light, Water, Magnetism, Movement, Temperature (Epigenetics)

Food isn't the only thing we . We also light. We also the temperature, the magnetism of the earth, and a few other things in our environment. How can this be? Because light from the sun is what sets our circadian rhythms, as well as provides numerous nutrients, including vitamin D, which we can't get from food. The Rewilder knows to follow the cycles of the day/night during their daily life. These lifestyle choices include avoiding artificial lighting and wearing blue-blocking glasses at night. It also means going to bed and rising with the sun, exposing ourselves to the sun in amounts that we require to get those frequencies that make us whole.

It means drinking pure living water, which is structured and energized by nature and also breathing the negative ions of air which have been purified and energized by the trees and atmosphere. It means not hiding from the season inside buildings that are over-insulating, over-protecting, and off-gassing toxins that wreak havoc on our immune systems. And lastly, it means wearing natural fibers that allow the skin to breathe and our body's energy systems to flow freely so we are grounded and connected to the environment.

To me, Primal, Paleo, and Ancestral Health should be considered an actual modality similar to Ayurveda, Chinese Medicine, etc. These principles are broken by modern views. The idea of veganism (eating no animal products) is only a product of over-domestication. Several generations have been cut off from rural farm living, where people lived off the land and relied on the same nutrition as their hunter/gatherer ancestors.

By raising meat, they were in touch with the processes of life and death. When cut off from that process, the idea of killing an animal for sustenance has become repulsive to some city dwellers. When, in fact, there is no traditional ancestral society that has been discovered that is vegan. Animal protein and fat are essential for human health and well-being. It is simple to see in biochemistry that plant protein is not adequate to build the thyroid hormone. So eating a vegan diet is like slowly starving our body as it becomes demineralized, and our metabolism becomes weaker and weaker…as mine did.

The proof probably won't always be revealed in the first generation. It is easy to see, even in photographs, the declining genetics experienced by modern civilization simply by seeing the narrowing faces as compared to previous generations.

It is well documented and easy to see how our ancestors enjoyed natural, robust wellness without a complex medical system. Weston A. Price first documented this in the 1930s. The foods they ate were in perfect balance with the requirements for metabolism. The diet was full of pro-thyroid substances, which provided the raw ingredients for perfect bone development and energy for coping with a rigorous lifestyle lived in the open air. Also, they did not have the hazards of modern life: artificial lighting, out of sync with the day/night cycles, out of sync with the seasons, disconnected from the earth's grounding due to living indoors, nonnative electromagnetic radiation coming from the electric grid, cell towers, and Wi-Fi routers, immunizations, polluted water, air, and soil, off-gassing of common household items, etc.

Nutrient-dense foods packed with the right minerals and vitamins amped up the metabolism, which warded off pathogens. Also, the act of moving around as hunter-gatherers, farming, and shepherding society is another essential nutrient that is encoded in our very DNA.

What's Wrong with the Standard Backpacker's Diet?

A few years ago, when I started the Ancestral (or Paleo) Diet, I could not find anything to take backpacking. All my life, I was taught that grains, nuts, and dried fruits were what you take for backpacking—the very things that were now on my "no-no" list. Also, things like granola bars and trail mix (nuts) are the standard foods that are mineral-depleting and hard to digest. These dried foods are easy to carry and prepare, yet they lack the nutrition to sustain the rigorous demands of living in nature. Many people return from long-distance hikes having lost large amounts of weight, showing their rib cages, and looking ragged. How can this be avoided?

I have personally spent the past twenty years on a mostly Paleo Diet and achieved a level of health I had never thought possible. There is a reason our ancestors were healthy and robust—practically superhuman compared to us. But what are the mechanisms for this?

Anti-nutrients and plant toxins

Grains, nuts, seeds, and many of our common fruits and vegetables can be harmful because they contain anti-nutrients. These are naturally occurring compounds in the plant but can have devastating effects on humans who eat too much of them. These anti-nutrients come in the form of oxalates, phytates, lectins, and aflatoxins. There are some other toxins as well, such as retinoic acid and polyphenols. Each of these blocks the absorption of certain minerals like zinc, iron, manganese, and calcium. Mineral deficiency is only the tip of the iceberg. Just about every known symptom, such as aches and pains, joint issues, eyesight problems, even brain fog and mood disorders, are possibly linked to plant or animal toxin poisoning. Some of these toxins also occur in animal foods, such as retinoic acid (vitamin A) and calciferol (vitamin D) found in the organ meats of animals, as well as dairy.

Sally Norton is a health coach, author, and public speaker known for her work on the health impacts of oxalates, which are naturally occurring compounds found in many plant foods. She has a background in public health and has focused her career on educating people about the potential negative effects of high-oxalate diets. Norton argues that excessive consumption of oxalates can lead to a range of health issues, including kidney stones, joint pain, and other chronic health problems.

Her book, *Toxic Superfoods*, explores certain foods commonly perceived as healthy and the hidden dangers due to their high oxalate content. Norton shares insights on how to identify and avoid high-oxalate foods, offering guidance for individuals looking to improve their health through dietary adjustments.

Sally Norton's basic philosophy centers on the idea that oxalates, naturally occurring compounds found in many plant foods, can be harmful to human health when consumed in excess. She argues that high levels of oxalates can lead to various health issues, including:

- **Kidney Stones.** Oxalates can bind with calcium to form crystals, which can accumulate and form kidney stones.

- **Joint and Muscle Pain.** Oxalate crystals can deposit in joints and tissues, causing pain and inflammation.

- **Gut Health Issues.** High oxalate intake can irritate the digestive tract and disrupt gut health.

- **Nutrient Absorption.** Oxalates can interfere with the absorption of essential minerals like calcium and magnesium.

- **Chronic Conditions.** Over time, the buildup of oxalates in the body can contribute to chronic health conditions and exacerbate symptoms of various diseases.

Sally Norton identifies several high-oxalate foods that she advises people to be cautious about or limit in their diets. Here is a brief list of some common high-oxalate foods she highlights:

- **Leafy Greens**

  - Spinach

  - Swiss chard

  - Beet greens

- **Nuts and Seeds**

  - Almonds

  - Cashews

  - Peanuts

- **Grains and Grain Products**

  - Buckwheat

  - Quinoa

  - Whole wheat

- **Legumes**

  - Soybeans and soy products (e.g., tofu, soy milk)

  - Black beans

  - Navy beans

- **Vegetables**
  - Beets and beetroot
  - Sweet potatoes
  - Okra

- **Fruits**
  - Rhubarb
  - Figs
  - Kiwi

- **Other Foods**
  - Cocoa and chocolate
  - Black tea
  - Certain spices (e.g., turmeric, cinnamon)

Norton encourages individuals to be aware of these foods' oxalate content and consider reducing their consumption, especially if they experience symptoms related to oxalate sensitivity or have health issues like kidney stones. Instead, she promotes a diet with lower-oxalate alternatives to improve health outcomes.

Ethics of Meat Eating

Factory-farmed meat is unhealthy and inhumane, unnatural, and far from Paleo. Don't eat factory-farmed meat. These animals are fed an unnatural diet of grains. However, pasture-raised organic meat is what was here before Europeans came and destroyed the land to create agriculture. Once, millions of bison roamed the Great Plains between Texas and Canada. Pasture-raised cattle are close to the natural ecosystem that existed before the advent of modern civilization. These grass-fed cattle live on land that often isn't tillable. Veganism is a product of over-domestication and a perversion of thinking that results when we are cut off from the cycles of life and death.

The mass exodus from the countryside to the cities during the Industrial Revolution led to losing touch with the cycles of nature and procuring one's own food. When everything comes from the supermarket, the connection to one's sustenance becomes remote and abstract. Also, the body no longer needs to know how to exist in the weather when surrounded by climate-controlled buildings and artificial lighting, which unyokes us from our circadian biology. Our instincts become shut down. Anyone who lives off the land would soon see you can't make it on grains and veggies alone. Even most fruits contain excessive plant toxins in the form of oxalates and reti-noic acid, which also lead to calcification of every tissue in the human body, oxidative damage, and aging.

CHAPTER 9

Food for Your Rewilding Journeys

Pemmican: The Primary Paleo Backpacking Staple

I kept hearing rumors about this mysterious thing called Native American Pemmican, and for many years couldn't find anything about it. Eventually things started showing up on the internet about its history and how to make it.

Pemmican was reported to be the primary staple for many of the tribes, especially the Plains tribes. Think about it—fresh meat would be available during a hunt, but not every day was a hunt. How would they preserve their meat without a refrigerator? Because of what I know about the health of these strong and proud people, I had an immediate trust in the power of pemmican to sustain energy and keep my body robust and ready for the rough and tumble lifestyle of my rewilder lifestyle.

So, what is pemmican exactly? Pemmican comes in many versions, but the basic components include pulverized dehydrated meat, melted fat, and spices/nuts/berries, all formed into a bar or paste. I didn't waste any time figuring out how to make it and started taking it on the trail with me. This ketogenic whole food was reported to have every piece of nutrition to keep you alive, well, and even thrive. It tasted a little weird at first, kind of dry and bland, but I learned to tweak the recipe until I got something that was beyond anything I had previously taken on the trail. I felt sorry for people buying pre-packaged dead foods and oatmeal. I couldn't imagine going back to that. This food has even passed the crowd-pleaser test. I have given it to friends completely unfamiliar with Paleo and they loved it. You can spice it in different ways to get a variety of flavors. You can use different fats like lard (rendered fat), coconut oil, and even butter for short trips or cold weather trips.

David Thompson, in 1810, described pemmican in detail, "…dried provisions made of the meat and fat of the bison under the name of pemmican, a wholesome, well tasted nutritious food, upon which all persons engaged in the fur trade mostly depend for their subsistence during the open season; it is made of the lean and fleshy parts of the bison dried, smoked and pounded fine: in this state, it is called beat meat: the fat of the bison is of two qualities, called hard and soft… the latter…when carefully melted resembles butter in softness and sweetness."

Meat drying on the rack.

As a backpacking food, pemmican is almost too good to be true. It has a practically infinite shelf life, weighs very little, tastes delicious, and doesn't even require cooking. Pemmican is the ultimate Paleo energy or meal bar. No amount of civilization can improve what was already perfect! My next step is to make food wraps made from beeswax and cloth, so I can avoid plastic altogether in my camping.

Each gram, if made with a fifty-fifty fat/lean mixture, is 6.5 calories, so each pound is 2,944 calories. You'd probably need seven to ten pounds for a seven-day trip, depending on your body weight and how hard you were pushing. This would be more than enough calories and would contain everything you need to not only sustain but even notice gains in lean muscle mass. You can supplement with whatever other foods you wish.

Pemmican is superior to jerky. Pemmican is jerky (dried meat), which is then pulverized and mixed with rendered tallow. You can add other ingredients as well. My favorite all-around recipe is:

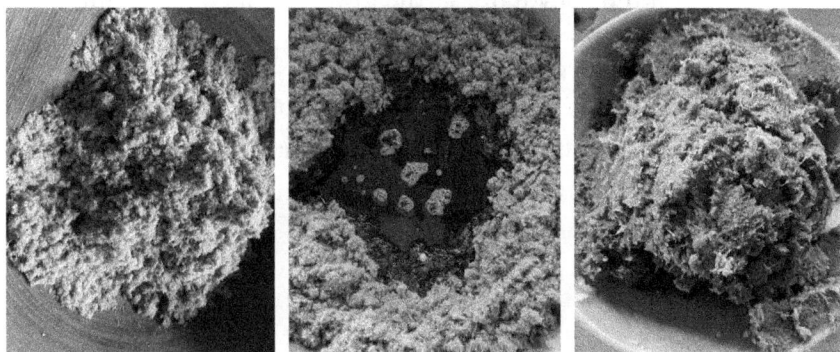

Pemmican Recipe

- 1 part dried and pulverized meat (humanely raised, grass-fed)

- 1 part tallow (humanely raised, grass-fed)

- Optional: sugar, honey, or salt

There are many varieties of pemmican. You'll need a food dehydrator. I recommend the Excalibur dehydrator and Vitamix blender to make it. If you want to do it the traditional way, you can pulverize the mixture by placing it in a cloth or skin bag and pounding it with a wooden mallet. You will see why the Native Americans call this "beat meat."

You can use either ground meat or sliced solid meat. Get the cheaper, less fatty cuts. The fat is an essential ingredient that we love, but it is best added after the lean meat is dried and pulverized. This will make pemmican with the best shelf life.

1. Place the meat on the drying rack. If using ground meat, spread it across the drying sheet and mash down with a fork to make it even (about half an inch thick). If using solid meat, slice meat into thin slices no more than one-quarter to one-half-inch thick. Place on the drying rack so they aren't touching each other.

2. Turn on the dehydrator at the lowest temperature setting (95 °F) and dry for about fifteen hours or until the meat is brittle.

3. Place pieces in Vitamix blender and pulverize. Don't let it get too hot. Push down with the mallet when needed. Fill Vitamix about three-quarters full. It needs to have enough in it to work.

4. Buy grass-fed tallow at the store or render the raw beef tallow by cooking it on low heat until it turns liquid (only takes a few minutes). Strain out the solid pieces, then let it cool to just above room temperature. The standard recipe is one part tallow to two parts pulverized meat. You can even use a 1:1 ratio, depending on your tastes.

5. Place the pulverized meat and other ingredients, such as berries, to a large mixing bowl and mix. Also, add salt and spices if desired. (Beware, some berries are high in oxalates, so avoid.)

6. Make an indentation in the middle of the pulverized ingredients. Into that, gently pour the liquid lard. Then, slowly mix the mixture with a large spoon.

7. Store in airtight glass containers. For travel, one option is to use reusable beeswax food wrap pouches.

8. This can be stored on the shelf or in the refrigerator if desired.

9. Enjoy as trail food or convenient energy boosting snacks!

More Paleo Backpacking Food Tips

Until recently, it wasn't easy to find packable animal-based foods that were ready for the trail. There are now several convenient grass-fed, ready-to-go primal superfoods. This menu is carefully chosen to exclude high oxalate foods such as seeds, nuts, and potatoes:

- Pemmican I make myself.

- Bone broth powder.

- A few farm or store-bought items: Honey, butter, cheese, dried fruit like dates, mangos, apples, bananas.

- Coffee (beware, green and black tea, as well as many herbal teas, contain excess oxalates).

- White rice, oatmeal, popcorn.

This menu proves to be delicious, energy-building, easy to pack and prepare, and easy to digest. It provides the strength and endurance needed for tough hiking. It is also good food for generating heat and for adapting to outdoor temperatures.

For most people, there will be a learning process of how to approach this diet: how much to eat, when to eat (and how often), and how to combine other foods with the pemmican.

Sample List of What I Would Bring per Person on a Four-Night Trip:

- Homemade Pemmican: 6 pounds (one pound per day per person plus a little extra).

- White Rice: 2 pounds (1/2 cup per person per day).

- Oatmeal: 2 pounds (1/2 cup per person per day).

- Raw grass-fed cheese:1/2 pound (optional and no longer recommended due to retinoic acid).

- Honey: 6 ounces.

- Butter: 1 pound (optional and no longer recommended due to retinoic acid).

- Dates, dried apples, prunes, bananas or other dried fruit: 1 pound.

- Fresh apples work well on shorter hikes.

- Bone broth powder: 6 ounces (no longer recommended due to retinoic acid).

- Coffee (four servings): optional.

It is a good idea to bring one or two extra day's worth of food in case of emergencies.

Backpacking Menu Plan

Typically, I eat three meals per day plus snacks. Each meal consists of my homemade pemmican as the staple. When hiking and camping, there is a greater need for calories as the exertion level is so high. So eating more often is normal for most people. Even eating during the middle of the night is often necessary.

Breakfast would include pemmican with a hot coffee and butter.

Lunch would be pemmican with some leftover rice from the night before, and some dried fruit.

Supper would include pemmican with rice, melted butter, slices of cheese and some dates for dessert.

Snacks would be carnivore bars, dried fruits, honey eaten directly from the silicon squeeze bottle, and maybe even popcorn for a special treat.

Especially because the food is dehydrated, I find it important to drink water in between each bite of food.

My typical backpacking meal has four parts:

1. A hot beverage and/or a hot soup

2. A starch such as rice or oatmeal

3. Pemmican

4. Pieces of dried fruit

I start by boiling a liter of water, which is used for either coffee in the morning or bone broth soup for supper. The coffee and soup each get a huge dollop of butter. It is best to mix the soups and beverages before leaving home and put them in labeled Ziplock bags. Or, to avoid disposable plastic, you can use empty pill bottles.

The pemmican (which is the primary nutrition of the meal) can be eaten separately, or it can be added to the soup at the end to warm it up. If you don't feel like starting the stove, you can always eat the pemmican by itself. It doesn't need cooking, but in cold weather, warm things are more inviting.

CHAPTER 10

Peak Performance Diet for Outdoor Adventures

Food can make or break any expedition because proper food is crucial to keeping the body going during rigorous adventures. I figured out how to bring Paleo foods on my backpacking trips and experienced phenomenal improvements in health and performance. Here, our bodies are challenged like nothing else in our day-to-day life. Also, during strenuous hiking and other outdoor adventures, the exercise itself aggravates the release of toxins from the liver and other tissues, which is why we feel sore from exercise. This is yet another reason to find a way to bring the body to a place of robust health without the toxicity that undermines it. The ideal I strive for is a hiking experience where I have phenomenal energy to take me to places I've never been without feeling depleted and run down at the end of the day or trip.

I had been practicing these Ancestral Health principles for about twenty years, and then I came onto some research showing there was more to the picture. This research, which was uncovered by Grant Genereux and Dr. Garrett Smith, was alarming due to strong evidence that this was problematic. New research shows vitamin A (a.k.a. retinoic acid) and vitamin D (a.k.a. calciferol) should not be considered vitamins at all but rather toxins. Furthermore, the effects aren't noticed early on, but they build up and accumulate in the tissue, especially the liver and kidneys. How could this be that after all this time of believing and practicing something I thought was beneficial and healthy, it was actually destroying me with a slow death?

Having a snack along the trail.

According to this research, these toxins and others get stored in our liver, and we can live a good life up to a point. But that ends when the liver becomes overly saturated, at which point we have symptoms that are all the symptoms of degenerative diseases. These can include bone loss, soft tissue calcium deposits, eye problems, aching and stiff joints, skin issues such as sensitivity to the sun, diabetes, arthritis, and many more.

This was flying in the face of what I had been doing and experiencing for two decades; however, I had a sinking feeling he was right, and I was wrong. Part of the reason for this sinking feeling was that I was having a lot of the symptoms he was describing. Even though the Ancestral diet had brought me to an amazing place of robust health like I had not seen before, where I could withstand harsh conditions and was in incredible shape, one thing, in particular, was still not getting better, and that was my eyesight.

Weston A. Price was the primary pioneer in looking for the root cause of disease and tooth decay (demineralization). One thing was evident: cod liver oil, which was taken to get vitamin A and Vitamin D, was actually hurting people. At first, Dr. Price advocated taking cod liver oil and eating organ meat, but later, he retracted that belief after more evidence came in about the problems it causes with accumulation.

The recent health movements such as Ancestral Health, Primal, Carnivore, and Paleo diets are all moving toward the best approach, yet none of these hits the mark like the recent Low Vitamin A diet. According to the Toxic Bile Theory, the best diet is Omnivore, which means some meat and some soluble fiber. The soluble fiber is needed to soak up the bile. The protein is needed to get the proper minerals and proteins, which create a healthy flow of bile. This is not an easy concept for most people to wrap their heads around. It requires some education to grasp the complex systems in action. These systems cause toxic bile to back up in the liver. This toxic bile then enters the bloodstream, wreaking havoc on all biological systems.

The Toxic Bile Theory was developed by Dr. Garret Smith and Grant Genereux. It posits that many chronic diseases stem from the liver's release of toxic bile into the bloodstream. An excess intake of vitamin A can contribute to this toxicity, leading to various health issues. To mitigate these effects, Dr. Smith advocates for a low vitamin A diet, emphasizing the reduction or elimination of foods high in vitamin A, such as liver, dairy products, egg yolks, and brightly colored fruits and vegetables. He also advises against vitamin A supplementation and the consumption of organ meats. By adhering to this dietary approach, he believes individuals can support liver health and reduce the risk of chronic diseases associated with toxic bile.

What Does a Low Vitamin A Diet Look Like?

The low vitamin A diet suggests avoiding foods that are naturally high in vitamin A, including both preformed vitamin A (retinol from animal sources) and provitamin A (carotenoids from plant sources). Below is a categorized list of foods to avoid:

Animal-Based Sources (High in Retinol)

- Liver (beef, chicken, pork, and cod liver oil are the highest sources)
- Dairy Products (milk, butter, cheese, yogurt)
- Egg Yolks
- Fatty Fish (salmon, tuna, mackerel)
- Fish Oils (cod liver oil, fish roe)

Plant-Based Sources (High in Carotenoids)

- **Orange and Yellow Vegetables**
  - Carrots
  - Sweet potatoes
  - Pumpkin
  - Butternut squash

- **Leafy Greens**
  - Spinach
  - Kale
  - Collard greens, Swiss chard

- **Fruits**
  - ♦ Mangoes
  - ♦ Papayas
  - ♦ Cantaloupe

Fortified and Processed Foods

- Fortified dairy and plant-based milk (many contain added vitamin A)

- Fortified breakfast cereals

- margarine and buttery spreads

- Processed foods with added vitamin A (e.g., meal replacement shakes, vitamin-fortified snacks)

Supplements to Avoid

- Multivitamins containing vitamin A

- Vitamin A and retinol supplements

- Fish liver oil supplements (like cod liver oil)

What to Eat on a Low Vitamin A Diet

- **Proteins.** Lean meat such as beef, bison, chicken, turkey, and lamb.

- **Soluble Fiber.** Rice, oats, barley, wheat, spelt, rye, and beans.

- **Vegetables.** Cauliflower, zucchini, and cucumbers (peeled).

- **Fruits.** Apples, bananas, and white grapes.

The Toxic Bile Theory suggests that reducing vitamin A intake may help the liver detoxify and prevent excess toxic bile from affecting the body.

Soluble fiber plays a crucial role in binding and eliminating toxic bile from the body. Here's how it works:

Binding Toxic Bile

- According to Dr. Smith, when the liver releases bile to aid digestion, it may contain toxins, excess vitamin A, and other harmful substances.
- Soluble fiber binds to bile in the intestines, preventing its reabsorption and ensuring it gets excreted instead of being recycled back into the liver.

Preventing Bile Reabsorption (Enterohepatic Circulation)

- Normally, the body reabsorbs up to 95 percent of bile salts to be reused.
- Soluble fiber traps bile, forcing the body to eliminate it and produce fresh, less toxic bile.
- This can help reduce the body's overall vitamin A burden and prevent its buildup in the liver.

Supporting Gut Health and Detoxification

- Soluble fiber promotes a healthy gut microbiome, which helps detoxify harmful compounds in bile.
- It also helps with regular bowel movements, ensuring that toxins and excess vitamin A leave the body quickly.

164

Reducing Bile-Induced Inflammation

- Some proponents of the Toxic Bile Theory believe toxic bile contributes to gut inflammation, leaky gut, and food sensitivities.

- Soluble fiber can help soothe and protect the gut lining, reducing irritation caused by bile acids.

Best Sources of Soluble Fiber (Low in Vitamin A)

If following a low vitamin A diet, good soluble fiber sources include:

- **Psyllium husk.** Metamucil, organic psyllium fiber.

- **Grains.** Oats, barley, wheat, spelt, white rice.

- **Apples** (peeled).

- **Bananas** (ripe without brown spots).

- **Legumes (small amounts, if tolerated).** White, navy, chickpeas, black beans, pinto beans, etc.

How to Incorporate Soluble Fiber in a Low Vitamin A Diet

- Take 1 tsp psyllium husk with water before meals to bind bile.

- Eat oatmeal for breakfast and white rice for supper.

- Consume peeled apples and bananas for snacks.

- Include small amounts of cooked legumes in meals.

Final Thoughts

In the context of Dr. Smith's Toxic Bile Theory, soluble fiber acts as a natural bile detoxifier. It helps the body eliminate excess vitamin A, toxins, and bile acids, reducing their potential harmful effects on the liver and gut.

Because of these new findings, I have changed my personal diet and my backpacking diet. Once I adjusted to the changes, the menu actually became much simpler and more satisfying. It is generally similar to the previously laid out plan, except now I omit dairy products like cheese, the high vitamin A fruits (mangos), coffee, and dried organ meats. I have added soluble fiber grains low in vitamin A, such as oatmeal and white rice, and some bread when possible. Over the few months since I've made these adjustments, I have noticed the improvements I was hoping for, such as better hiking performance, less soreness, better sleep, and improved vision. This has been my journey, and I share it here so each of you can decide what you want to try.

I realize this paradigm is so new that many people will not want to consider it because it will contradict many previously known principles and viewpoints. Most people are still in the phase of trying out the Paleo and Carnivore approaches. It can be difficult to let go of the immediately noticeable improvements for the idea that relief of symptoms can be caused by stopping the detox pathways. Eventually, when things build up enough, the liver can no longer store the toxins and bile gets released into the blood from a process called cholestasis. This toxic bile leaking into the blood can be traced to probably all chronic and even acute diseases and symptoms. There are so many theories, diets, and explanations for disease and root causes that one can get lost and confused easily. It is hard to know which paradigm or practice to follow or try. I am only putting this information here as educational material in case the reader may want to pursue this further via the low vitamin A communities found online.[7]

---

7   https://ggenereux.blog/wp-content/uploads/2016/10/extinguishing-the-fires-of-hell2.pdf And nutritiondetective.com

PART 4

Camping Basics

167

CHAPTER 11

No Trace Camping

No Trace Camping, a.k.a. Leave No Trace, is a set of ethics that every camper should be familiar with and adhere to. These practices and philosophies ensure your safety as well as protect the wildlife and other campers from possible dangers. When in the wilderness, there is a new approach to sanitation and social etiquette because we don't have modern facilities.

1. How do we pee and poop in the woods?

- **Peeing:** Urinate at least two hundred feet (about seventy steps) from water sources, trails, and campsites to avoid contamination.

- **Pooping:** Dig a cathole at least six to eight inches deep and two hundred feet from water sources. After use, cover the hole with dirt and disguise it with leaves or rocks. In some areas (like deserts or alpine zones), you may need to pack out your waste using a WAG bag (waste disposal bag). Always check local regulations.

2. How do we keep our food from attracting animals?

- Store all food, trash, and scented items in a bear-proof container (bear canister) or hang them at least twelve feet high and six feet from the trunk of a tree using a bear hang system.

- Cook and eat away from your tent (at least two hundred feet) to avoid attracting animals to your sleeping area.

- Never leave food unattended, and don't store food in your tent.

3. How do we deal with leftover food scraps and trash?

- **Pack it in, pack it out.** Carry all trash, including food scraps and wrappers, out of the wilderness with you.

- Strain dishwater and scatter it away from camp to prevent food odors from attracting wildlife.

4. How do we leave the campsite the way it looked before we got there?

- Avoid altering the campsite—don't dig trenches or move rocks unnecessarily.

- Use existing campsites and durable surfaces like gravel, rock, or dry grass to pitch tents.

- Scatter any natural materials (like sticks and pine needles) that were moved.

5. What is proper etiquette when encountering other parties on the trail?

- Yield to uphill hikers—they have the right of way.

- Step aside and give space to horses and pack animals.

- Keep noise levels low to respect the wilderness experience for others.

6. How do we wash our bodies, clothes, and dishes without polluting water sources?

- **Use biodegradable soap sparingly**, and always wash at least two hundred feet away from lakes, rivers, and streams.

- Scatter wastewater rather than dumping it in one place to minimize impact.

7. How do we keep from trampling the vegetation?

- Stick to established trails and campsites to minimize damage.

- Walk single file in the center of the trail to avoid widening paths.

- In fragile ecosystems (like alpine meadows), walk on rocks rather than plants.

8. How do we have a fire without leaving a trace?

- Use a camp stove instead of making a fire whenever possible.

- If fires are allowed, use established fire rings and keep fires small.

- Burn only small sticks that can be broken by hand and burn everything to white ash.

- Scatter cool ashes and return rocks or logs to their original places.

By following these principles, campers can help preserve nature for future generations while ensuring their own safety and enjoyment.

Bear Protocol

Proper bear protocol is crucial when camping in bear country to ensure the safety of both humans and bears. Most of these practices also apply to other animals, such as raccoons, mice, etc. Here is a bulleted summary of the key considerations and practices included in the "no trace camping ethics" when it comes to bears:

Preparation

- Research the specific area you will be camping in to understand the types of bears (e.g., black bears, grizzly bears) present and their behaviors.

Obtain any required permits or information from local authorities or park rangers regarding bear safetyFood Storage

- At all times, when not engaged directly in cooking, keep food strung up in a bag at least ten feet high and ten feet from any branch. Use bear-resistant containers, a.k.a. "bear canisters," to store all food, garbage, and scented items (toothpaste, soap) when not in use.

- Use a bear canister in areas that require it or if it is an area without available places to hang the food bag. Store this bear canister at least fifty feet away from camp.

- Cook and eat away from sleeping areas to prevent food odors from lingering around your campsite.

- Do not use scented lotions on your body.

Cooking

- If using a campfire, do not burn food waste in it. The smell will linger in the ashes.

- Cook and clean up away from your sleeping area.

Bear Encounters

- Make noise while hiking to alert bears to your presence, reducing the likelihood of surprising them. You can bring a whistle. This is especially helpful when going around blind corners.

- One option is to carry bear spray and know how to use it. Keep it readily accessible and easy to reach, not buried in your backpack. Alternatively, there is a device called the Siren, which puts out a bright flashing light and loud noise.

- If you encounter a bear, remain calm and speak in a calm, firm voice. Back away slowly without turning your back on the bear. Also do not look the bear directly in the eye.

Hiking

- Hike in groups when possible; bears are less likely to approach larger groups.

- Stay on established trails, avoiding dense vegetation where bears might be harder to see.

- Keep children and pets close and under control.

General Camping Ethics

- Pack out all trash, including food scraps and litter, to leave no trace of your presence.

- Avoid burying or burning food scraps, as bears have a keen sense of smell and can easily locate buried food.

- Do not approach, feed, or attempt to interact with bears or any other wildlife.

Remember that bear behavior can vary depending on the species and individual bears, so always stay informed and adapt your practices accordingly. Be prepared and exercise caution to minimize potential bear encounters and promote the safety of both humans and bears in bear country.

CHAPTER 12

Backpack Basics

Backpacking is both an art and a science, demanding careful consideration of engineering principles when carrying all essentials for the upcoming days on your back. The volume and weight of each piece of gear, equipment, and clothing should be thoughtfully evaluated, with a preference for items serving multiple purposes. The choice of a backpack is critical, and its size must align with your specific body measurements, particularly the torso length.

Selecting the Right Pack

1. Torso Length Measurement

- Determine your torso length, measured from the top of the shoulder down to the top of the hip bone. You can use a string holding one end at the top of your shoulder and the other end at the beginning of the hip bone.

- Typical torso lengths: 17" (small), 18" (medium), 19" (large).

- Purchase and test your pack well in advance of your trek.

- Be familiar with adjustment straps for efficient use.

2. Weight Distribution

- The right-sized pack is the beginning of correct weight distribution and symmetrical placement of gear.

- Most weight should be felt on the hips, with shoulder straps securing the upper pack to prevent movement.

- Hip belt tightness is crucial for efficient weight transfer to the hips.

3. Organization and Accessibility

- Tuck away cords, straps, and dangling clothing.

- Wet clothing can be attached to external straps for drying while hiking.

- Quick-access items should be strategically placed in easily reachable pockets.

Gear Organization

1. Laying Out Gear

- Lay out all gear and categorize it into piles or stuff sacks (cookware, toiletries, first aid, clothing, sleeping gear, food).

- Utilize Ziplock or resealable bags for efficient organization and moisture protection.

2. Packing Strategy

- Place light gear at the bottom and use designated compartments for items like sleeping bags.

- Heaviest items, such as food and cooking utensils, should be close to your back.

- Outer pockets can be used for frequently accessed items like snacks and water bottles.

3. Weight Considerations

- Aim for 25 to 30 percent of your ideal body weight.

- Base weight (pack without food and water) should ideally be around twenty pounds or less.

- Checklists in this guide can help achieve weight goals.

4. Compression Straps

- Tighten all compression straps to prevent gear shift and discomfort during the hike.

5. Final Adjustments

- After securing the backpack, tighten the shoulder, hip, and sternum straps.
- A well-packed backpack transfers weight to the hip belt, reducing strain on the shoulders.
- Regularly readjust straps during the hike for optimal comfort.

Efficiently packing your backpack not only ensures a more enjoyable hiking experience but also minimizes the risk of discomfort or pain upon reaching your destination. Proper gear organization and weight distribution are key to a successful and comfortable backpacking journey.

The Lucky Sheep™ 65 Liter Backpack

I have designed a backpack from organic canvas and treated it with water repellant beeswax formula. This pack offers comfort, style, and technical performance all at once.

The breathability, ruggedness, and grounded feeling of canvas is unparalleled, even with today's high-tech synthetic options. This is a very simple design, and yet highly technical and effective.

This backpack features a different type of strapping system. The cross-chest strapping system is more ergonomic than the standard over-the-shoulder straps because it frees up the shoulders from having a heavy strap pulling on them with each stride. The shoulders are not a good place to place the load because the shoulders should be free for walking.

In addition, this cross-chest strapping system provides a type of "pivot technology." As you take each step, the pack moves less and thus saves energy. When you need to bend down, duck, or crawl, this pack hugs your body better than any other.

This all-natural twenty-ounce pack uses a minimalist design where the primary gear is placed inside the body of the pack. First, place your closed cell foam pad around the inside circumference to create an internal frame system, or fold it onto the inside back section. Then, place a sleeping bag, clothes, and other gear inside that. Use the three outside pockets for items that can get wet, such as a tent, water bottles, and cooking gear.

The top extension allows room for food and fuel for several days. When not using the top extension, the lower portion of the pack is fifty liters.

The Canvas Backpack 65 L also features adjustability galore.

1. Start with getting the correct size according to your torso length.

2. Then, use the main body cinch strap to tighten the overall pack.

3. Then, pull down on the shoulder strap, cinch straps, and hip belt.

4. Then, tighten the top lift straps to pull the pack closer to your body.

Proper fit customized to what happens to be in your pack and snuggled up to your body results in more comfortable and efficient hiking.

CHAPTER 13

How to Choose the Right Campsite

Avoid widow-makers. Widow-makers are dead limbs sticking out of trees above you or trees leaning over and not solidly rooted. These limbs and trees might fall and injure you.

Look for good air circulation. Look for a spot that doesn't have a lot of undergrowth. If there is thick undergrowth, the spot can be prone to mold. Closed areas with lots of undergrowth hinder air circulation. On prairies and deserts, there is usually no problem here, but in a forest, you want to look for areas with tall trees and not a lot of undergrowth.

Look for good water drainage. Don't pick a low-lying, flat place that might become a pond. A slight slope is good. Or a spot slightly raised above the immediate surrounding area. You can often tell where the water will pool or run by studying the ground. Be aware of and avoid places where water can rise without warning, such as arroyos.

Ultimate places to pitch a tent. These are next to waterfalls, streams, and lakes. Summer is the ideal time to camp at the top of a mountain, and in winter, be sure to camp in places protected from the wind. This usually means lower down and protected by trees or land formations. Stagnant air creates microclimates that foster mold. The most vitality is from the fresh air continuously circulating into the area. The most auspicious place for air quality is next to moving streams.

Protection from EMFs and geopathic stress. If you don't feel well at a campsite, it may be due to geopathic stress. This is either a ley line or an underground water stream, which can weaken the body. Some people use muscle testing or other methods to check on the suitability of a campsite. If you notice something uncomfortable or have trouble sleeping and don't know how to dowse, simply shift to somewhere nearby. Even a few feet can make a difference.

Protect from insects. Camp near moving water when possible, which naturally repels biting insects. Another place that is likely to be free of insects is the top of a ridge, especially in spruce-fir forests. You can use a stand-alone net tent under a tarp if your tent doesn't already have built-in netting. I also carry a bottle of oregano, eucalyptus, and lemongrass essential oil and apply it when needed. For instance, if there are a few mosquitoes trying to land on my face, often they will go away once I apply some of the essential oil. My favorite brand is Herbal Bug-X from North American Herb and Spice. Alternatively, I carry a piece of no-see-um netting and place it over my face, sometimes propped with my umbrella.

Avoid wind tunnels and exposed ridges when winter weather is possible. Find a place down away from the ridge to set up camp.

Wilderness etiquette, privacy, and safety. As much as possible, you want to be in a place where no one knows you're there. Making camp at least two hundred feet from a trail is the proper etiquette for Leave No Trace camping. It is considerate of everyone to keep as low profile as you can and let everyone experience the wilderness and solitude they came to get. It is also good etiquette to keep contact and conversation with strangers to a minimum for the same reasons.

Stealth camping is setting up in as minimal a way as you can away from the established campsites. However, there are some public places that require you to stay in designated campsites and use only existing fire rings. Still, you can use a lot of these techniques in those places, too.

Insulating against the cold of the ground and preventing condensation in your bedding. When sleeping on the ground, you need to watch for condensation on your bedding materials from moisture. When moving camp every day, you solve this by airing out the sleeping bag, ground cloth, and tent whenever possible. But when staying in a more permanent camp, there are two basic methods.

1. Use a slatted wooden bed frame (even the Native Americans practiced this). This can be constructed by putting multiple, even diameter limbs side by side. One can use anything from willow shoots to standard hardwood trees such as poplar and pine. This falls more in the category of bushcraft, and you will, of course, need tools such as a saw and hatchet for this.

2. In a wilder place, make a bed by piling leaves or other debris to create a leaf mattress. Cover that with a tarp, which could be synthetic, or it could be canvas oil cloth or animal skin (fur). It depends on how wild you want to be.

How to Pitch a Tent in the Rain

- Take off your pack.

- Remove the tent/tarp and ground cloth, which should be on the outside pockets of the pack easily accessible.

- Pitch the tent and place the backpack inside.

- Get in and take your wet clothes off. Replace with your dry base layer, etc., which is secured in a waterproof bag inside the pack.

- Get in your wool sleeping bag if you need to warm up after cold exposure.

Sleep Tips

Cover the Eyes and Ears

Earplugs (silicon) and cloth (bandana) or articles of clothing over the eyes. Since you don't have a room or cave to block the light and sound, you can create a sanctuary this way. This is a personal preference because some people don't like doing this for one reason or another. I find I sleep deeper, especially when there is loud crashing water nearby, wind, rain pelting my tarp, or loud crickets and cicadas. Sometimes, I also practice listening to the sounds and merging with them as a sound meditation. It can be delicious to really hear the sounds as though they are a symphony. Other times, I don't hear any sounds at all, even though they are there. It is fun to be aware of our consciousness and how our perceptions are always shifting.

Inclined Bed Therapy

Find the right slope, no greater than eleven degrees, and place your head on the uphill side. This is about a six-inch rise from head to toe. This actually enhances circulation and lowers the heart rate because the heart works less than when lying flat. This enhances sleep and dreaming. It is usually easy to find these slopes when in the mountains and usually easier than finding a flat spot. I also recommend creating a sloped surface at home to sleep on. Not only is it better for your health and sleep, but it will also condition you for your wilderness trips.

Pillow

Make a pillow using extra clothing articles alone or stuffed into a stuff sack.

CHAPTER 14

A Rewilder's Day
Hiking Checklist

When it comes to wilderness preparedness, the phrase "think positively" doesn't apply. Instead, this is one time the best practice is to think negatively. That is, consider all the possibilities of what could go wrong on a hike. Then, using a checklist, make sure you have covered all the bases. You can hit the trail with confidence because you know you are ready for anything.

The Ten Commandments of Hiking

A set of ethics and principles has been developing among hikers and mountaineers which to this day has not changed a lot for decades. These standards are taught in outdoor leadership schools as hallmarks of a safe and enjoyable trek. The idea is to think through the trip and ask, "Can I prevent emergencies and respond if I need to?" If the answer is yes, then the next question is, "Can I safely spend a night outside if I have to?" Make a checklist of all the possible things that could go wrong. Do you have what it takes to deal with each emergency or prevent it in the first place? Do you know what action steps to take for each of these?

Don't fool yourself. Hiking in the wilderness is not a walk through the park. Wishful thinking is a product of over-domestication where we aren't used to fending for ourselves. Out beyond the trailhead, it is just you up against nature. How can you think through every possible scenario of an emergency? It is well established that they are cold and wet (hypothermia, frostbite), sun (heat stroke, sunburns, glare), sprains, fractures, burns, cuts, bites, blisters, bugs, bruises, and stomach upset. There are established ways to approach all of these situations, and the standard protocols are a good place to start. However, there are also a few more effective things that I have added, using herbal first aid, energy medicine devices, and clothing/shelter that follow the principles of Rewilding.

These carefully selected items should be considered and gathered ahead of time and kept together in a place that is ready to go. Because to be essentially prepared is quite more extensive than simply throwing a few things in a bag and taking off. I haven't always followed these guidelines. I have had several life-threatening outings without being properly prepared. One of these, I ended up bivouacking (spending the night without a tent) in a pile of leaves on the edge of Mount Mitchell in temperatures that dropped to near freezing. I have learned from experience to make sure I have the ten essentials and not to worry about the extra weight of items that may be rarely used. Consider it your survival insurance policy.

The Ten Essentials

1. **Navigation.** Map, altimeter, compass, GPS device, PLB, satellite communicator, or satellite phone, extra batteries or battery pack.

2. **Headlamp.** Plus extra batteries.

3. **Sun protection.** Sunglasses, sun-protective clothes, and sunscreen.

4. **First aid.** Includes foot care and insect repellent (if required).

5. **Knife.** Plus repair kit.

6. **Fire.** Matches, lighter, and tinder, or stove as appropriate.

7. **Shelter.** Carried at all times (can be a lightweight emergency bivy).

8. **Extra food.** Beyond minimum expectation.

9. **Extra water.** Beyond minimum expectation or the means to purify.

10. **Extra clothes.** Sufficient to survive an emergency overnight.

List of Everything I Carry on a Day Hike

1. Navigation

- Phone with GPS software for navigation (covered in Ziplock bag).

- Paper map and real compass (phone may not always work).

2. Headlamp

In the outdoors, headlamps are the flashlight of choice, freeing hands for anything from cooking to climbing. The efficient, bright LED bulb has completely replaced the inefficient incandescent bulb of a few years ago. An LED bulb lasts virtually forever but batteries do not, so always carry spares. If you are using a rechargeable headlamp or batteries, start with a full charge. Any headlamp carried by an outdoor shop will be weatherproof, and a few models can survive submersion. All models allow the beam to be tilted down for close-up work, such as cooking and pointed up for looking in the distance. Some headlamps feature a low-power red LED to preserve night vision and help climbers avoid disturbing tent mates during nocturnal excursions.

3. Sun Protection

- Sun-protective clothing.
- Wide-brimmed crushable wool hat.
- Coconut oil-based sunscreen with zinc oxide.

4. First Aid Kit

5. Knife

- Use it to make kindling as well as other things.

6. Fire

- Flint and steel with cotton in a waterproof container and/or lighter or matches.

7. Shelter

- Silnylon tarp and ground cloth (two pounds).

8. Extra Food

- Pemmican, dried fruit (extra ones not intended to be eaten during the trip, but for backup only.

9. Water Filter

10. Extra Clothes

- Sweater.
- Merino base layer (top and bottom).
- Wool socks.

Stuff I Take for the Hike Not Included in the Extra Preparedness List

- What I am wearing: Shoes, wool socks, merino wool shirt, wool pants or shorts (varies with the time of year).

- Lunch and snacks.

- Water.

- Rain parka.

- Wide-brimmed wool felt hat.

- Winter: I would include mittens, hat, crampons, and often a stove to heat water.

This information is also used for multi-day backpacking treks.

It is only a short step from packing for a real emergency preparedness day hike to a backpacking trip. The main difference is that there would be more food, cooking utensils, clothing, and a sleeping bag.

Further Tips

The same first aid kit can be used at home and kept in the car for trips. For a short hike, I take a watered-down version in a small pouch. Avazzia without the attachments, Oreganol, waterproof tape, and cloth gauze.

The Avazzia microcurrent machine takes the place of many other herbs and medications, thus making the load lighter. For instance, no need for ice or heat. Also, there's really no need for arnica cream or homeopathy because the Avazzia takes the place of each of these. Of course, you can still use these, and from experience, you will learn just how to combine the different treatments.

It's easier to keep one first aid kit because keeping one in good order is about the only practical thing that works. Batteries run out, and supplements expire.

I save empty pill bottles to use for holding small amounts of remedies. Also, it is important to label everything.

It's a good idea to take some wilderness first aid training.

CHAPTER 15

A Rewilder's Herbal First Aid Kit

Here is my checklist for what I put in my herbal first aid kit:

First Aid Kit

- Waterproof wrapping tape.

- Gauze (or pieces of wool or linen fabric).

- Oreganol tincture from North American Herb and Spice: This is wild oil of oregano in a mixture of olive oil. This is essential for venomous bites. Also, a few drops on your skin will keep most bugs away.

- Some kind of fat-based ointment or simple tallow (for wound care).

- Ground flax seed to mix with activated charcoal and/or bentonite clay for venomous bites as a poultice.

- Activated charcoal.

- Aspirin.

- Moleskin for blisters.

- Butterfly bandages as an alternative to stitches.

- Needle with silk thread for stitches.

- Tweezers for removing ticks and splinters.

- Lugol's Solution (iodine) for purifying water.

- Avazzia Biofeedback Energy Device (optional).

- Cloth wipes (in Ziplock).

- Paper and pen (for messages and record keeping if needed).

Natural Treatment for Venomous Snake and Insect Bites

Embracing the principles of Rewilding involves immersing oneself in nature without relying on modern medical assistance. In such situations, knowledge becomes a crucial tool, potentially saving lives and instilling confidence. Surprisingly, the most effective approach to treat venomous snake bites involves the use of herbs, specifically echinacea tincture or oil of oregano. Unlike conventional treatments typically found in first aid kits, these herbal remedies are vital for immediate intervention, as waiting for anti-venom treatment at a hospital may prove too late.

In the absence of modern medical help, having knowledge about natural remedies becomes paramount. Among the recommended herbs, wild oregano oil and echinacea stand out, with a preference for oregano oil due to its efficacy. Notably, these herbs extend their benefits beyond snake bites, proving effective for treating other insect bites, sprains, cuts, and even bruises.

How It Works

Our bodies consist of individual cells held together by hyaluronic acid, akin to the mortar that binds bricks. Venom from snakes and spiders, such as rattlesnakes and hobo spiders, contains an enzyme (hyaluronidase) that liquefies the hyaluronic acid, leading to severe tissue damage. Similarly, certain bacteria produce this enzyme, causing infections that may result in tissue loss.

Oregano oil and echinacea play a crucial role in preventing and repairing the damage caused by this process. Echinacea contains a chemical that inhibits the destructive enzyme while also stimulating the body to produce more hyaluronic acid, facilitating repair.

Treatment of Venomous Snake Bites

Take internally one half-ounce of either oil of oregano or echinacea tincture every fifteen minutes with water for two hours, then every four hours. Soak the affected area with the chosen herb immediately after the sting or bite to prevent venom spread. Follow this with a drawing poultice consisting of slippery elm bark powder, activated charcoal, bentonite clay, apple pectin, and turmeric powder, applied externally to draw out toxins and aid in wound healing.

Preparation and Kit

It is crucial to prepare a kit in advance, including oregano oil, a drawing poultice, homeopathic remedies, gauze, plastic wrap, and tape. This kit should be readily accessible during outdoor activities like hiking or camping, ensuring a prompt response in case of a bite or sting.

Bruises and Sprains

For soft tissue injuries, internally take oil of oregano or echinacea tincture, and apply externally. Arnica cream and pills, along with aspirin, can also be beneficial. The drawing poultice formula can be used internally for stomach upset and food poisoning.

In conclusion, understanding the properties and uses of echinacea and oregano oil can be a lifesaver in the absence of immediate medical assistance. Preparing a kit with the necessary components ensures a swift response to venomous snake or insect bites, promoting safety and well-being in natural settings.

CHAPTER 16

Overcoming Fears

As part of my rewilding journey, I spent over two years sleeping and living outside, both in a tipi and on wilderness excursions. During this time, I developed a spiritual/psychological reset where nature became my default place to be. It also required me to find a way to be at home in different locations…like a nomad. I used breath awareness and meditation to connect with my heart center and pull myself into the present moment. This was extremely useful because before I learned to do that, I would be associating a place to return to as home.

What I noticed is that my relationship with the forest changed. The main occurrence I felt was a kinship with animals, plants, the earth, and weather. I could feel the aliveness of the forest. It wasn't a boring bedroom with four walls and total predictability. In the wilderness, things are in constant flux, like weather, day/night cycle, animals, and terrain. The ground is uneven. There is no furniture other than the occasional boulder, which happens to be the perfect shape for a chair or a tree limb to perch on. There are no buildings to protect from temperature and weather extremes. Also, it is pretty easy to have unpleasant things happen like sunburn, bug bites, bruises, sprains, poison ivy, hypothermia, or simply anxiety from fear of the dark or things that go bump in the night.

Anyone can overcome the fear of being vulnerable in nature. It mostly takes practice, and it helps to have someone with experience show you the way. Find friends or join a hiking club or Meetup Group.

Cultivate a Relationship with the Animals, Plants, Earth, Weather, Dark, and Being Alone

This is where the WILD enters your REWILDING lifestyle. This is the wilderness, and we are re-establishing a relationship with it. There are bears and other critters out there who can harm us, and we need to be prepared by knowing what these are and how to avoid confrontation.

However, the majority of situations do not pose a serious threat, and people have coexisted with wildlife since the dawn of humanity. Most of these fears are like the fear of the dark or the fear of being alone...mere fears.

The psychological aspect of fear is where the soul meets the ground. There is only one way to cure oneself of these fears, and that is by facing them, challenging them, and finding that they are not a problem. All of us outdoor veterans have gone through this process, and many a campfire circle is spent relating our war stories. At first, every little twig snapping is cause for alarm. Then you realize you are out here living with all these creatures, and it is okay. You are out on the living earth, sharing it with all the other animals and insects and creating a relationship with nature, which before was cut off behind closed doors.

When I first slept in a wild area without a tent, I spent most of the night unable to sleep. I felt so exposed and vulnerable and not safe. But that one night proved to me nothing was going to happen. That's about what it takes for most of us. I have spent so much time outdoors I have learned how to relax and feel protected in nature. Some people put up a protective shield or bubble and set the intention that nothing will enter. Use whatever tools work for you! Again...this is exactly why we are doing this. Because for generations, humans have had a fear of nature and have launched an all-out war to dominate her. And now we are discovering we want to reconnect.

Animal Encounters

I have had many nights of animal encounters, such as deer, owls, coyotes, bears, foxes, and even frogs. (Yes, one night, sleeping near a stream, some frogs jumped on top of me as they were making their way back to the water.) I usually sleep either in an open tarp or under the open sky. What I found out is the animals actually give me space and, in general, are not a threat.

After so many encounters, I now relax around the whole teaming wilderness and feel like my space is respected. I feel like I earned this respect by dropping my fear. This happened by me facing my fears and challenging them one by one. We humans don't realize how we live our lives in pretense. We hide behind our machines, appearance, identity, accomplishments, and buildings. We live our lives through our identities (egos). There is no way to see this until we step outside.

Many years ago, I was in a near-death experience. I was lost on Black Dome, the highest mountain on the East Coast, at night in October and survived by piling up some leaves to crawl under. After that, I was humbled to feel how little I am in the eyes of the mountain and nature.

In the beginning, it was really scary to be walking through the forest at night. It seemed like a thousand eyes were watching my every move. And actually, there probably were and always are. Out there, you can hide nothing. In nature, truth has no barriers. Your thoughts become amplified, and you see your life clearly, and perhaps that is the biggest fear of all—the fear of being alone.

PART 5

Rewilding Lifestyle for Strength, Longevity, and Being Ready to Go On Backpacking Journeys

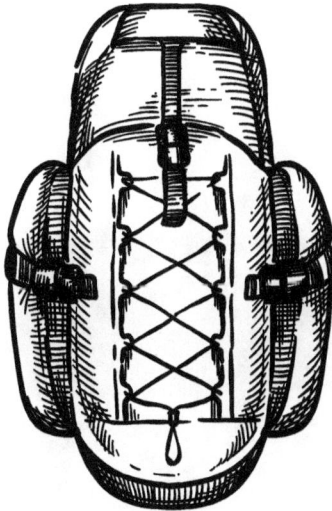

CHAPTER 17

Things You Can Do at Home

When I take my friends camping, they are amazed at how easy I make it look. I just whip out my gear, have the tarp up and every-thing organized no matter the weather, and usually fall asleep as soon as I hit the sleeping bag. I have spent many years trying to find a way to be more comfortable outdoors. My goal was to make it feel like home. What I mean by that is that I want to feel relaxed, safe, and comfortable. After all, I came to nature to get closer to my primordial existence. So, wouldn't it make sense to feel more at home?

The barriers to reaching that place were many. It has taken me years to reach my goal, which was to easily transition from indoors to outdoors as if there were not that much difference. I use my everyday lifestyle to train for the outdoors. This is how I have built an outdoor body and mind ready for the rigors of the wilderness.

Our over-protected, over-padded, over-domesticated, and over-processed culture pushes nature out. If we design our indoor environments and lifestyles with rewilding in mind, we will be half-way there before we even get to the trailhead.

Learn and Practice Sleeping with a Minimalist Environment at Home

This means a firm surface such as the floor or a slatted wooden bed frame. Sleeping on a firm surface at home will prepare us for the transition when we venture into the wilderness.

Primal Sleeping Fundamentals: Where the Body Meets the Surface

For thousands of years, humans have slept on minimal surfaces without mattresses. In only a few decades of corporate propaganda and advertising, people have come to think of sleep and mattresses as practically synonymous. However, what we don't know is mattresses are robbing us of the deep sleep that we would more easily find with a more simple and primal sleep environment and surface.

I believe the reason mattresses have become ubiquitous is mainly due to these reasons:

- The perceived comfort is an adaptive response. The body becomes front-loaded due to factors such as chair sitting and mattresses. When the body stretches and lengthens on a firm surface, those tight muscles and ligaments are stretched and noticed, causing discomfort.

- The psychosomatic aspect of a mattress: It looks thick and plush and therefore it must be comfortable.

- Since mattresses have been around for so long, no one even questions their usefulness. Therefore, no studies are performed.

- The propaganda of a century of advertising.

Sleeping on a Firm or Hard Surface Benefits and Techniques

- Relaxation response and deeper sleeping are created by the synergy of all these factors:

- Alignment (natural kickback mechanism of breathing action against sleep surface which re-aligns the body as you sleep).

- Increased breathing capacity and oxygenation of blood.

- Increased circulation.

Techniques for Adapting the Firm Sleeping Lifestyle

- Bodywork remediation.

- Body awareness and ability to relax all muscles evenly against the surface so no pressure points are felt.

- Propping and positioning the body in ways unique to this kind of surface.

After a lifetime of mattress use, you are probably going to feel uncomfortable when you first start sleeping on a firm or hard surface. And what is meant by a "hard" surface?

I have personally tested various beds, futons, and natural surfaces over several decades and have come to the conclusion that what mattress manufacturers call firm or hard does not even come close to the traditional Japanese futon. What describes this quality best is a thick quilt on a floor or board. That bit of padding (about one to two inches of compressed padding) won't let the hips sink in to misalign the spine, yet it buffers the bones somewhat. From my own experimenting and interviewing people, I have come to the conclusion that this amount of firmness is what works for most Americans who are changing their lifestyle and sleeping habits.

You will need to experiment for yourself to see what works. You can start with napping and later try sleeping this way. It may take more than one night to get used to it. You can gradually go to a harder surface and compare the results. The interesting thing I have found upon informally interviewing people who have tried sleeping on firm surfaces is that they complain about it being hard and less comfortable, and yet they sleep very well and feel refreshed upon awakening.

You can sleep on a platform bed or on the floor. A platform bed is a simple raised surface where your mat goes, but it does not have a true mattress. The platform bed is best for those who don't want to get down to the floor level.

The Japanese use a tatami mat under the futon. This provides ventilation underneath which helps regulate body temperature as well as keep the futon from becoming damp with the body's perspiration. It also keeps the futon, blankets, and pillows off the floor, which might be dirty and drafty. This is a great invention but is expensive and doesn't always fit in with a person's interior design. A simple tatami mat imitation can be easily handmade from lumber. All that is needed is a slatted surface raised a few inches off the floor. Or the platform bed can serve as a tatami mat if it has a slatted surface.

Further Sleep Tips

If possible, sleep on your deck, porch, or tent in the yard. Keep windows open as much as possible and the room as cool as possible. The best sleeping is freezing winter nights under enough layers of wool, as I found out during my tipi days, which I still practice to this day.

The Main Tricks to Make Sleeping on a Firm Surface Comfortable, Easy, and Enjoyable

- When sleeping on your side, extend the bottom leg straight out, bend the knee of the top leg, and extend it over the bottom leg.

- When sleeping on your back, place a rolled-up sock in the small of your back.

- Make a pillow by placing extra clothing in your stuff sack. For side sleeping, the pillow should keep your head level with your shoulder so that the shoulder is fully extended. If there is no pillow, then keep your bottom arm extended, and your bicep becomes your pillow. For back sleeping, the pillow should be adjusted smaller and placed only at your neck so you have cervical support and traction that decompresses your neck and doesn't push the back of the head up.

I don't believe in hammocks for night sleeping unless it is for some reason, such as there is no level ground or you need protection from ground crawling insects. The reason is that hammocks tend to bow the back, which hampers breathing and alignment, thus compromising sleep. I also don't like air mattresses in general. But if someone has a special need, injury, or mere preference and it makes them happy, so be it.

When backpacking, I use a closed-cell foam pad. Although this is synthetic, it is the only thing I know of to date that is really practical for outdoor adventure. In the old days, they would have used a piece of tanned animal hide with fur on (which is similar to the felted wool pad).

Learn Constructive Primal Movement

Our push-button society has taken the healthy movement out of our lives. There is not an opportunity to sit on the floor, squat, kneel, crawl, or stretch in all the many ways we would be if we were hunting and gathering. Movement is required for us to remain healthy, flexible, resilient, strong, supple, and maintain a healthy range of motion and mobility. Backpacking is a great way to bring this movement back. However, it is good to have some training so you don't carry unhealthy patterns with you. There are many schools for this, and it is easy to find instructions online. Some suggestions include the Feldenkrais Method, Alexander Technique, yoga, MovNat, ecstatic dance, etc.

The Primary Primal Movements We Need Outdoors

- Walking. Yes: walking. We don't do this right. You can find excellent videos on YouTube.

- Getting up and down to the ground (sounds simple, but chances are you have no idea how to do it constructively).

- Squatting (this is the perfect resting position and also for pooping and peeing).

- Lying down (it sounds crazy, but we can't even do this right).

- Crawling, ducking, and bending down.

Training Tips

- Wear a loaded backpack and go on day hikes. This will develop balance and muscles that you would otherwise not be using.

- Get used to the clothing and shoes you will be wearing.

- Sleep in your yard or porch in order to test your gear and adapt to the cold.

- Go on short day hikes to test your gear and skills until you feel confident.

- Learn to use a hiking map application on your smartphone as well as a paper topo map and compass until you feel confident with your navigation skills. You can even use this to go around the block or on trips in the city, just for learning purposes.

- When you are at home and there is severe weather, use that as an opportunity to go on short outings to test your gear and clothing. For instance, camp in your yard or a nearby park during a blizzard.

Shakedown Trip — Testing All Your Gear and Food Items

Go on a short overnight trip before embarking on a longer trek. Make sure you like the way everything is working. This is called a shakedown trip. Take notes and create your own checklist of what you are going to bring on your bigger adventure.

CHAPTER 18

The Art of Carrying Things

When you have to carry belongings on your back or in your bicycle bag, you look at what you own in a new way. You develop more of an appreciation for the object and what the object does for you. If it isn't worth its weight, you are more likely to get rid of it or not acquire it in the first place. We develop a more intimate relationship with the things we must transport, and this teaches us to live as light and free as possible. This is one of the things we discover when hiking, backpacking, or bicycling, where minimalism shines.

The human body tends to atrophy without adequate use. Weight-bearing exercises such as walking and lifting strengthen not only the muscles but the bones as well by causing calcium to be deposited in the bone.

Here is an excerpt from *Indian Basketry* by George James:

Dr. Hudson once saw an old woman carry three bushels of potatoes in this manner through rain and mud to her home two miles distant. Greater loads are not unusual to the men, and as a consequent result of such customary labor, the Poma Indian is abnormally developed in the dorsal and the anterior cervical muscles, besides having a chest magnificent in proportions. This applies also to the Calivilla, the Havasupai, Paiuti and other Indians, who, like the Poma are accustomed to carry large burdens on the back with the carrying band over the forehead.

The human body is designed for movement. More than half of the body's muscular equipment has as its primary function walking. When we sit, the top-heavy head and shoulders are constantly pulled forward by the force of gravity, and the flexible S-curved spine is hard put to keep its shape against this steady, distorting pull. The muscles that hold all these movable parts in their proper relation to one another are under constant tension. Standing still is also an uncomfortable position. Notice how your body sways forward and backward with gravity and fatigues quickly, causing you to find something to lean against.

A study was published in 1971 that investigated seven different ways of carrying a load of 30 kilograms for 1 kilometer at a speed of 5 kilometers/hour. The results of this study verify why native people prefer to carry things in three ways: on the head or in baskets strapped to the forehead or shoulders.

In Carolo Castenada's *Journey to Ixtlan*, there is a scene where Carlos has come to visit don Juan, and don Juan asks him where his writing gear is. This scene illustrates the body awareness that is inherent in native peoples (as well as the negative social stigma held in Western Society, which is associated with carrying items on one's back).

I had left my notebooks in my car. Don Juan walked back to the car and carefully pulled out my briefcase and brought it to my side.

He asked if I usually carried my briefcase when I walked. I said I did.

"That's madness" he said. "I've told you never to carry anything in your hands when you walk. Get a knapsack."

I laughed. The idea of carrying my notes in a knapsack was ludicrous. I told him that ordinarily I wore a suit and a knapsack over a three-piece suit would be a preposterous sight.

"Put your coat on over the knapsack," he said. "It is better that people think you're a hunchback than to ruin your body carrying all this around"

Of course, Carlos was only doing what he had been trained to do in Western society. But according to the above-mentioned study, carrying a load in the hands is the most inefficient way to do it, using 6.96

kilocalories per minute (for a weight of 30 kilograms) as opposed to the back from the shoulders (4.83 kilocalories per minute), a basket on the head (4.90 kilocalories per minute) and a basket on the back suspended from the forehead with a tumpline (5.54 kilocalories per minute).

When a weight is carried, the normal erect posture is modified so that the center of gravity of the lifter plus the load approximates the center of gravity of the lifter alone. This is why people lean forward when carrying a backpack. The trunk functions as a counterbalance, altering its inclination so that the projection of the center of gravity at the feet remains relatively constant. Carrying the weight close to the body makes it easier to balance as well as turn around.

A tumpline is a band of cloth or skin about two inches thick, strapped across the forehead (or higher on the head), and attached to a basket or other object, which rests against the back. The basket or carrying vessel can be a variety of shapes and sizes. Conical seems to be a popular shape as it forms a wedge that holds most of the weight up high where, with leaning, the body's center of gravity is balanced.

The modern backpack is the height of the evolution of carrying baskets, combining principles of age-old technology plus some very recent improvements.

Features of an Industry Standard Modern Backpack

- Streamlined design.

- Fits snug to the body.

- Cinch straps to tighten the payload when needed.

- Distributes weight efficiently/evenly.

- Water repellant.

- Generously padded hip belt and shoulder straps.

- Sufficient pockets and compartments to organize gear efficiently.

- Expandable so it can carry a small load (50 L) or a large load (65–80 L) when needed.

- Rugged but also lightweight.

- Some kind of pivot technology which allows the backpack to stay somewhat centered when the hiker is leaning.

Don't Let the Mountain Kick Your Ass

Prepping for the Trekking — A Full Body Workout

Backpacking is an extreme sport. The physical exertion is unlike almost anything in daily life. Your entire body is suddenly thrust into carrying a heavy load it's not accustomed to on uneven terrain and often with extreme elevation changes. Every thousand feet of elevation gain or loss adds the equivalent energy expenditure of walking an extra mile on flat ground. That means a two-mile flat hike burns the same calories as a one-mile hike with one thousand feet of elevation change.

Calories Burned with Different Loads and Elevation Gains (B&W Friendly)

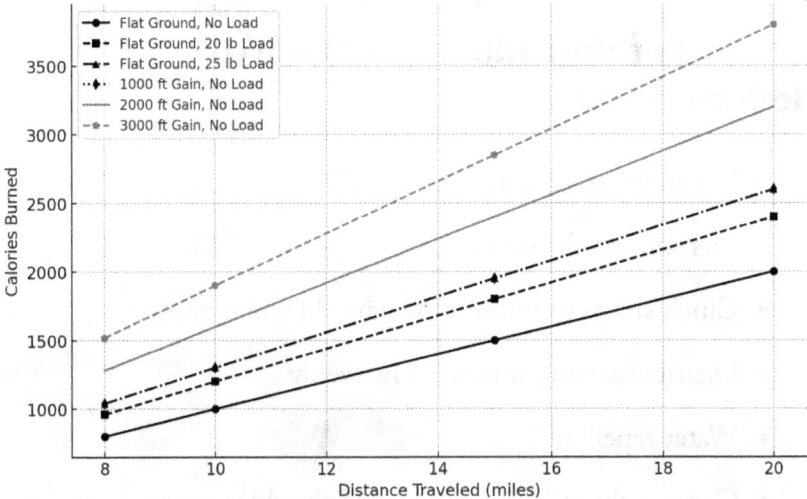

- Flat Ground, No Load
- Flat Ground, 20 lb Load
- Flat Ground, 25 lb Load
- 1000 ft Gain, No Load
- 2000 ft Gain, No Load
- 3000 ft Gain, No Load

Calories Burned

Distance Traveled (miles)

Planning a backpacking trip requires calculating how much time and energy it will take to get from camp to camp. Any weaknesses or imbalances in your body will be revealed—and can ruin your trip. So, how do you prepare? How do you avoid getting your ass kicked by the mountain? The answer: proper training.

The Right Kind of Training

Sure, lifting heavy at the gym helps. But for a rewilder, daily training hikes make way more sense. Even if you live in the city, putting on your loaded pack and walking around a park trains the exact muscles you need. Plus, you're getting sunshine and fresh air—key parts of the circadian rhythms balancing lifestyle.

Training hikes also let you dial in your backpack fit and test your clothing. Don't let bad weather stop you—see it as a chance to test your rewilding gear before hitting the trail. When the time comes for your real trek, you'll have full confidence in both your body and equipment.

Strengthening Your Feet

If you're rewilding your feet, this is the perfect time to train with minimalist shoes or even go barefoot. This strengthens your natural alignment and foot muscles, which are essential for longer treks. If you're new to barefoot shoes, start without carrying a load. The extra weight is for advanced rewilders.

A Free, Full-Body Workout

This training isn't just for hiking—it's the ultimate full-body workout, and it's free. Plus, if you're hiking in the woods, you get the added benefits of forest bathing—reduced stress, improved mood, and enhanced well-being.

A Simple Training Plan

Try this one-hour-per-day workout to build strength for the mountains.

1. **Choose Your Trail or Route.** Find a local trail or loop.

2. **Pack Your Pack.** A weekend backpacking load is around 20 to 25 pounds (9-11 kg). Start lighter if needed.

3. **Go on Your Daily Hike.** Aim for at least three to four times per week.

4. **Increase the Load.** Add more weight gradually—water bottles work great for this.

5. **Test Your Balance and Gear.** Train on uneven terrain. Consider using trekking poles for added stability. Walk up and down stairs to mimic elevation changes.

6. You can add extra miles on weekends when you are ready for more. You can add extra weight even if it is more than you plan to carry.

Once you can hike comfortably for an hour with your target pack weight, you'll be ready for the real deal.

Fueling for the Trek

As you train, you'll naturally start eating more to support muscle growth and energy demands. This helps you calibrate your food intake for the trail. Pay attention to how much you eat now so that when it's time to pack for a trip, you'll know exactly how much food you need.

Recovery and Longevity

Your body will need maintenance. As you build strength, incorporate massage, yoga, foot rehab (rollers), saunas, and hot baths to relieve sore muscles. Over time, this routine will make trekking in the mountains with a heavy load feel effortless—you'll hit the trail with a skip in your step and a smile on your face.

CHAPTER 19

Cold Adapting with Ancestral Health Practices

Cold thermogenesis refers to the body's ability to generate heat in response to cold exposure. This practice, widely embraced by the Ancestral Health community, offers numerous benefits—both physiological and psychological.

Most people instinctively avoid the cold, staying indoors or seeking warmer climates. But before you shudder at the idea of enjoying the cold, hear me out. What if you could feel warm in freezing temperatures—without relying on modern heating? What if you could experience a deep sense of well-being by aligning your body with natural circadian rhythms? Once you adapt, winter can become energizing rather than something to endure. You may even lose the urge to escape to the beach.

For years, I struggled with winter. As a vegan, my hands and feet were always cold, no matter how many layers I wore. But everything changed when I switched to a Paleo diet—specifically, what I call "Circadian Balanced Paleo." I began generating a natural, radiant warmth from within. Eventually, I started spending time outdoors shirtless, walking barefoot in winter, and even jumping into freezing rivers—for fun.

Cold Exposure Supercharges Health

Cold exposure is both a stressor and a powerful tool for strengthening the body. Here's how it enhances overall well-being:

- **Increases mitochondrial efficiency.** Improves cellular energy production and metabolism.

- **Enhances cell communication.** Cold optimizes quantum biology, piezoelectricity, and semiconductor activity, allowing cells to transmit signals more effectively.

- **Activates heat production (thermogenesis).** Converts fat molecules into cellular energy, warming the body.

- **Synchronizes circadian rhythms.** Signals the brain to hibernate, improving sleep quality.

- **Boosts metabolism and burns fat.** Stimulates the thyroid, turns white fat into brown fat, and helps the body become leptin-sensitive, improving fat-burning efficiency.

- **Supports detoxification.** Releases stored toxins from fat cells, pushing them to the liver for processing.

- **Reduces stress hormones.** When done correctly, it lowers cortisol and adrenaline, promoting relaxation.

- **Increases resistance to cold over time.** With adaptation, shivering decreases, and the body retains more heat naturally.

Why Most People Struggle with the Cold

Our modern lifestyle disrupts circadian biology, making it harder to handle cold temperatures. The body gets "tricked" into thinking it's always summer, which creates imbalances in metabolism and heat production.

The three biggest culprits:

1. **Poor Diet Choices.** Many people follow a diet mismatched to their climate. The Ancestral Food Pyramid flips the standard FDA pyramid upside down, prioritizing meat and saturated fat over carbohydrates.

Carbs (sugars, fruits, grains) are designed to fuel tropical environments—they burn quickly into energy without generating heat. In contrast, saturated fats (butter, tallow) provide slow-burning energy while releasing heat. A glucose molecule produces 36 ATP (cellular energy), while a saturated fat molecule produces 147 ATP—more than four times the energy!

That's why eating seasonally matters. While you can consume out-of-climate carbs in moderation, reducing them in winter will optimize your body's ability to generate warmth.

2. **Overheating and Artificial Environments.** Constant exposure to heated indoor spaces, artificial lighting, and non-native EMFs (electromagnetic fields) mimics summer conditions and confuses the body's natural adaptation process.

To counteract this:

- **Spend time outside daily.** Even in cold weather, even with minimal clothing.

- **Reduce indoor heating.** Especially at night, to support circadian alignment.

- **Limit blue light exposure.** Use blue-blocking glasses, red light bulbs, or candlelight in the evenings.

- **Limit exposure to non-native EMFs.** Which disrupt biological signaling and increase cold sensitivity.

3. **Wearing the Wrong Clothing.** Most modern clothing is made from synthetic fibers, which disrupt piezoelectric energy flow along the skin and trap moisture, interfering with the body's heat exchange system. Wool, however, functions like natural fur, allowing better heat regulation.

How to Train Your Body to Generate Heat Naturally

1. Eat an Ancestral Diet

- Prioritize meat and saturated fat for long-lasting energy and warmth.

2. Gradual Cold Exposure

- Take a daily walk in a T-shirt for at least twenty minutes.

- Try barefoot walking, even briefly, to stimulate adaptation.

- Increase cold exposure gradually—listen to your body's limits.

3. Reduce Indoor Heating

- Turn down or off the heat for periods of time.
- If needed, keep just your bedroom cooler for better sleep.

4. Block Artificial Blue Light at Night

- Use IRIS software to filter blue light from screens.
- Wear blue-blocking glasses or use red-light bulbs in the evening.

5. Follow Natural Sleep Cycles

- Sleep as much as your body needs—winter is a natural hibernation period.
- Wind down early and avoid artificial stimulation at night.

6. Switch to Wool Clothing and Bedding

- Wool acts as natural insulation, unlike synthetics.
- Wool blankets allow you to breathe inside for additional warmth.

7. Stay Active with N.E.A.T. (Non-Exercise Activity Thermogenesis)

- Avoid sitting for long periods—stand, stretch, or move frequently.
- If you work from home, integrate short bursts of movement (yoga, push-ups, jumping jacks) throughout the day.

8. Incorporate Heat Therapy as Needed

- Take hot baths or use an infrared sauna to help regulate body temperature.
- Layer up in wool blankets for passive heat generation.

My Journey with Cold Adaptation

After years of struggling with the cold, everything changed when I adopted a Paleo diet. My body began radiating heat naturally, and my outdoor tolerance increased dramatically.

Inspired by historical accounts of Native Americans thriving in winter with minimal clothing, I experimented with gradual cold exposure. As I adapted, I found myself craving cold—walking barefoot in the snow, taking ice baths, and eventually, moving into a tipi for the winter to put these principles to the test.

At first, my fingers would go numb within minutes. After two weeks, my circulation improved, and I could move my fingers normally—even in freezing temperatures. My body was rewiring itself, optimizing my metabolism for winter survival.

The Science of Cold Adaptation

U.S. Army research from the 1960s found that men exposed to 50 °F (10 °C) for eight hours a day became cold-adapted within two weeks—they stopped shivering, maintained body heat better, and burned fuel more efficiently. Similar studies confirm that all humans have the ability to acclimate to the cold.

What About Frostbite and Hypothermia?

Cold adaptation must be done gradually and safely. If you push too hard or too fast, you risk dangerous cold exposure. To warm up after a session:

- **Use a sauna or hot bath** to bring your core temperature back up.

- **Go on a brisk hike** to generate internal heat.

- **Try the Wim Hof Method** of breathwork techniques that generate body heat.

Final Thoughts

Cold adaptation isn't just about survival—it's about thriving. With the right diet, exposure, and lifestyle, you can reawaken your body's ancestral resilience and experience winter in a completely new way.

Are you ready to embrace the cold? Start small, listen to your body, and enjoy the adventure.

PART 6

Nature and Consciousness

CHAPTER 20

The Mystical Powers
of Moving Water

The Schumann's resonance, if you recall, is also the frequency of the alpha brain wave state, which induces coherent heart rate and relaxation response.

There is another electrical field created by moving water, such as streams, creeks, and waterfalls, where water crashes over rocks. Even underground water has a charge and that is what dowsers find when they are looking for wells and other underground features. As water moves along the surface or an underground channel, it creates an electric charge by the force of friction.

I noticed this many years ago, and I had no words or concepts. I just felt instantly relaxed when next to moving water. However, I noticed that moving water, especially creeks and streams crashing over rocks, had a strange healing and detoxing effect. I wasn't sure if it was physical, spiritual, or both. All I knew was when I spent too much time around unhealthy places, people, and situations, I could go to a creek or stream to camp, and I would be recharged very quickly beyond anything I could imagine.

Normally, when we are confronted with conflict and trauma, we run away from it and seek a pleasant experience to cover it over. I had practiced Zen and Vipassana Buddhism as well as Transcendental Meditation for decades. This was the core teaching. This is what creates inner conflict and suffering in each of us. We aren't happy with what is; we want to move toward what feels pleasant and move away from what doesn't feel pleasant. I had recently discovered a new mystery school with a set of teachings that went even deeper. In this school, which was based on Hindu teachings and led by Avatars Sri Kalki Amma Bhagavan, there were processes that allowed temporary states of higher consciousness. This was instigated through certain sadhanas (spiritual techniques), which opened the chakras and allowed the flow of Kundalini. These temporary states of Ananda (bliss consciousness) also cleared samskaras (or previous trauma experiences that are held in our memory). There was a whole new energy opening up inside me.

These processes were bringing up buried feelings and experiences which had been too painful to process. These went all the way back to childbirth and even before. There was an exquisite deliciousness to the experience and, at the same time, a feeling of intense pain and grief. It was as though the pain and grief by itself would be too much to handle, but by freeing up a little of the stuck energy in the body's memory, it could be felt and released.

This would happen over and over again in layers. I went through a process of midlife crises where I was processing my entire life, which led up to the present. What seemed like a life of failure that ended in feeling disconnected from myself, friends, family, and everything, I was letting go of seeing myself as the story of what I had accomplished or failed at or the progression of events I had experienced, or the belongings I owned, or the place I lived, which before had created my identity.

In between these sadhana processes, I craved nature like never before. I couldn't get enough of the ground, the trees, the sky, the sound of the stream, and alone time. These were my solace and my sanctuary. Nothing had ever felt so good. This whole process had taken my life for a turn I had never anticipated.

While I was enjoying the lusciousness of the forest, all the sweet aromas of dirt and flowers and the cacophony of wind and chirping birds, I was having a feeling of ease and joy without replacing one experience on top of another. I wasn't running away from anything but was going to nature to confront myself and be with the experiences I was having.

All this was part of what is called a kundalini awakening. What this means is that point where a person realizes the whole of their life has been to bring them to a place where identification doesn't come from the things of the temporal, mundane, or material world. The complete, true essence of experiencing life rather comes from aligning with something deeper than one's life journey, accomplishments, relationships, struggles, and victories.

In the words of my teacher, Sri Kalki Amma Bhagavan, "Until we are free of the mind, we are only existing, not living."

Instead of seeing myself as "my story" that got me from birth to where I was, I was seeing that none of that was really me. And in that, there was a death process happening. And that death is actually the act of dying to one's psychological self. As I experienced the old way of being in the world dying, I needed something to assist me beyond the yogic processes. Because I would go very deep into a process and come out and be disoriented. Because there was no old self left to orient to. For instance, I could no longer talk about the past. And if someone brought up the past, I would not be able to relate to it anymore. It would be like seeing a movie of someone else with no emotional attachment to the situation and not even recognizing the main character who once was me. So now, what do I do with no compass? There was no me. There were only feelings of deep bliss mixed or followed by feelings of terror or what spiritual masters call the void. Or visa versa.

As I was discovering this, I started experimenting. I noticed I could have a different reaction to the exact same camping spot in the forests where I live at different times. Normally, it worked like this: on the first night of camping, I needed maybe fifty feet to get the right feel where I was getting the soothing therapy of the stream. If I was closer, it would feel harsh, and I couldn't relax and sleep well. But usually, the next night, I would feel good up next to that same water. I would set my sleeping pad as close to the water as I could get, with my head almost touching the water. I imagined the water was cleansing my aura…the energy field around my body. And if I arrived with a lot of chaos and conflict in my consciousness, it would need a gentle coaxing to smooth it out. Then, once I was cleansed of the surface debris, I could get in closer and get a deeper effect. At some point, the water was penetrating the depths of my soul to wash out the negativity or experiences from the past that were traumatic and not serving me.

These memories are stored in our body. Sometimes, they are called muscle memory, tissue memory, or samskaras. I could let the water go all the way into my bones and restructure me with its own pristine Divine Source energy.

As the water tumbles down the rocks, it creates turbulence, which actually purifies the water. Rocks can be considered as "filters;" although they don't actually filter in the normal sense of the word, rocks do, however, purify the water, which is the same end result as filtering. However, in addition to purifying the water, meaning making it free of toxic substances such as chemicals and waterborne pathogens, the water crashing over rocks also becomes more energized. This energy can be measured in the form of light energy. Tap water becomes unstructured, which means the water loses its crystalline structure. When this happens, the water cannot enter the cells of our body, and we become dehydrated.

However, perhaps the most important aspect of water is that it has memory, and it records everything it comes in contact with. Experiments done in many countries of the world have shown that water receives and makes an imprint of any outside influence, remembering anything that occurs around it. Anything coming into contact with the water changes the water.

Water molecules cluster together, and these clusters record the whole history of their relationship with the world as if on magnetic tape. As water acquires new properties from this memory, its chemical composition remains unchanged. Science has come up with ways to measure water, and this has allowed us to show the mechanism of how it works. Within each of water's memory cells are 440,000 information panels, each of which is responsible for its own type of reaction with the environment.

We all know that the human body is composed mostly of water. To me, that would explain a mechanism for how our bodies store what is called muscle memory. To me, that would explain a lot. That's partly how we absorb the vibrations in our environment. And so it would follow that being exposed to pure water in nature, which has been energized by the forces of nature, including rocks and turbulence, and through the negative ions in the air, we would be absorbing these pure frequencies perhaps on multiple levels. Also, as we listen to the sounds and expose ourselves to the frequencies, the water inside our body also starts to vibrate with those coherent waves.

I would drink the water, swim in the water, listen to the water, and feel the sun in contrast to the cold. I would surround myself with the water on many levels and be intensely present with it and myself. The detoxing effects of this moving water would be erasing the memory in my body, which was partly perhaps stored in the form of the water in my body. So, as I was sleeping several hours beside the stream or creek, the cells of my body would start resonating with that pure frequency. As that happened, the impure memories stored with their old frequencies of hurt and trauma would start to be released. And that would form a type of detox reaction, which could be felt on several levels, including physical, mental, emotional, and spiritual planes. As the memories leave, they would sometimes bring themselves to the surface of my consciousness, and I would feel them. There would often be periods of intense confusion, grieving, and pain followed by a renewed sense of boundless and causeless joy. Just a feeling of lightness. What the Vedas call Sat Chit Ananda is our true nature beneath all the layers of personality and thought. This means ultimate reality and true freedom is the experience of truth, consciousness, and bliss and is not dependent on a story or identity.

My friend, who has electromagnetic hypersensitivity, explained to me that she could not sleep by water because it aggravated her sensitivities. I explained to her my theory about how I felt the moving water creates its own electric charge, and since she has an electrical engineering background, she got it completely and could explain it even in her own terms. "The dose is the cure," she said. She has started sleeping further away from it to get some of the cleansing benefits and then slowly moving closer toward it, increasing the dosage as needed. As we all rewild our bodies, minds, and souls, we need more tools like sun, trees, rocks, and moving water to assist us on our journey.

Some Personal Experiences with Consciousness Shifts

Journal Entry from September 2013

I went alone into the wilderness for three days to be by the river, and the river was giving me deeksha (divine blessings) constantly and bringing up everything into the light. Every truth in my life was up in my face, and I could see into the past and the future. It was hard to be with, but if I stayed with the things coming up, they would work through me and pass on. It was an intense sadhana (spiritual practice). It was like amplifying all the hidden corners of my consciousness, shedding light, and presenting me with the truths I was walking with. I mean truths about myself and my relationships. Truths about how I cannot create stories to hide me from other stories. Showing me where I had fear and where that fear was blocking the flow, creating resistance to life and to what is. Like one example is my life as a whole and how the whole arch has come around to what it is today. And what is today is the result of a lifetime of events, relationships, actions, etc. And I could let all that just melt into one big acceptance. I could see the power of everything. And I could see how I was involved in it and how I am not involved in it now. How even though it happened, and at one time I experienced certain emotions, those events and lessons just passed on. There is no substance to them. They are not me and have very little to do with me. And the trauma that resulted was washing away in the light of this awareness.

In fact, the residue that is there from the emotional imprint was now cleansed by the power of grace and of the river. However, if I believe in those things and believe they are me, they continue to live in me. And I was in a hyper-release mode during this time. I was letting things come up, a massive life review, and letting each thing burn and pass on. There were no distractions. No person to talk to and bring me out of this intense inner exploration. No book or computer. Only observing nature in its primordial state. Only the roar of the river, changing with each moment. Only the shapes of the trees against the sky or the endless variety of formations of boulders and rocks worn smooth by centuries of pounding water.

Journal Entry from July 2, 2013

The spinning solar plexus chakra dream/vision I had by the stream a couple of weeks ago has really been revealing itself. At the time, I had no idea what it meant, but what's turning out is it means a complete reset of my consciousness. It is like a solar plexus prescription or a washing out of my conditioning. The conditioning that has set this life into motion so far is going out the window. It is scary because it involves walking on the razor edge between trust, faith, surrender, guidance, and constant reassessing to see if ego or Divine Will is driving my actions and motivations. There is nowhere to rest except the present moment and all that is whatever currently happens to be running through me at the time, so it's just plain crazy. Crazy because there is nothing to fall back on except frequency. I can tap into frequency and get calmed down, but not a story about how I think of my life or me as a person. There is no reference point like home, job, or relationship. I mean, it would be nice if there was, but in my case, I don't want to use these things as reference points. I don't want my family or job or places I've lived to be reference points. It's just because

I find no meaning in those. I mean my family, for instance, there is meaning there, but it is not in some kind of history. It is the meaning of standing in my own present truth and seeing what I see. That is the meaning and not something that happened when I was seven, and therefore, this is how things are. There is no shared comradery in saying, "Remember when _____ did such and such when we were babies, and you got mad and cried." It's completely pointless, and I find myself not being interested in conversations…at least from that level. I can still carry on a conversation, but there is no one there talking. The words and images just go through me in both directions. But this often leads to some critical point of consciousness shift, which is where I become very interested. I have seen my relationships transform like crazy right before my eyes. People will confess something that has been bothering them their whole life or apologize or talk about something at a deep level that we had never before accessed.

CHAPTER 21

Confessions of an Accidental Shaman

A few years ago, I had an urge to live outside so I would become comfortable being in the wild. There wasn't even much of a goal to it...but I was simply drawn to spend as much time in the wild as possible. The only way to do this practically was to set up camp near the places I would go for work. I would spend part of the week at my house in town and spend the other half of the week at a place where I worked on the edge of a national forest. I would sometimes stealth camp, meaning no-trace overnight camping. Other times, I would set up a base camp in the Pisgah National Forest and bring my laptop computer and enough rewilding gear and supplies to spend a few days writing. I enjoyed quiet time in this outdoor office space, surrounded by the sound of the stream and the fresh scents of flowers.

Part of the time, I was searching for poles for my new tipi life; part of the time, I was working on my laptop; and part of the time, I was testing my ideas with outdoor gear made from natural fibers. During this period, I was basically undergoing a complete life reboot (i.e., midlife crisis), and I developed an amazing relationship with animals, which unfolded gradually.

My Early Forest Bathing Retreats Using Natural Fibers

One place I frequented was known for bear activity. I slept either under the open sky or using an open tarp. It was weird at first because

I felt like I was sharing the same bedroom with all kinds of other beings. The atmosphere was alive with energy and always changing, unlike the dead space of a modern bedroom with solid walls and a roof. The sounds were, at times, unnerving. I could be walking to my camp in the dark, and suddenly, strange and sometimes eerie sounds would come out of the darkness. I would little by little sort out just what animal was doing it and the type of behavior or communication it was making.

After some time of living this way, I started wondering why I didn't have any encounters with bears. I felt at that point that the animals in this area knew me and gave me space. After having spent a year or two visiting this area and camping under my magical grandmother pine tree by the babbling brook, I was part of their community. I grew less and less apprehensive as I spent more time there. I kept my food safely tied ten feet up on a limb according to proper protocol.

I would often get up in the morning and start my day with a bath in the icy stream. One morning, I was sitting on the rocky bank facing upstream, and I saw a bear cub playing in the water, completely unaware I was there. After a while, it jumped up on the bank, and I believe it spotted me. That told me I am surrounded by these beings, big and small, and they are allowing space for me. There is nothing to fear.

As I became more of a part of the forest, I also noticed my superpowers seemed to be increasing, not just around animals. Once, I was near a Native American burial site on the prairie, and I woke up to voices shouting in a Native language and another sound that resembled an organ playing a strange grating off-pitch chord, which drove me to get on my bicycle and pedal back to my mother's house (I was visiting) in the middle of the night, a few miles away.

I sometimes heard coyotes, and they were often very close. They go into a hideous howling frenzy, which raises the hair on my back. I haven't heard coyotes actually attacking a human, which is partly why I tried to relax around it. In fact, I knew a cowboy-type guy who, many years ago, once woke up to a coyote licking his face while he was sleeping under a bridge. So I just let myself adjust to being alone with coyotes nearby and obviously aware of me.

There were times I heard terrible sounds of what I believe was an animal being attacked and killed, probably by a fox. Other times, I've heard a fox coming down the trail toward me (making a sound like a woman screaming), and then when it got within a few feet of me, and I yelled out, it screamed again and then silence and then I heard it again far down the trail running like crazy.

I also started doing a little experimenting with attempting to make animal sounds. I started with owls, and I learned I could actually call back to a barred owl, and it would call back to me. I could do this repeatedly, and I was baffled…did it think I was an owl, or was it just curious what it would be like to talk to a human?

My experiences got weirder and weirder. I know that my totem animal is the eagle or thunderbird. I had many experiences when I was younger with lightning, which is associated with the eagle, such as the time a tree was struck by lightning, and an official Native American shaman confirmed with me at one point that the eagle is my totem. I could hardly believe it because it is basically the highest totem a person can have. A person with eagle power is highly revered and seen as a leader. Because the eagle soars high, seeing the whole picture, it is, therefore, the most powerful and far-seeing. Well, the funny thing is, after this animal initiation period, I was seeing eagles everywhere, even in the city. I would look up, and no sooner there would be an eagle flying. I had to warn my friends, "We may see an eagle. Don't fear." It happened so regularly that sometimes they were very high and sometimes flying just above tree level.

When I lived in the tipi, they would fly right over my tipi often. One day, I was driving down the road, and the corner of my eye caught what might have been an eagle circling up above. I stopped at my favorite skateboard parking lot, which is part of a little country church near my house, and I saw an eagle circling slowly, not very high, toward me. I was riding my skateboard around the parking lot and stopped when it got closer and just watched it. This amazing bald eagle circled slowly just above tree level immediately around me. I was mostly in awe but also a bit fearful, not exactly sure what was going on. This amazing bird, which is my very totem, was telling me, "Don't worry…we've got your back."

Carolina Wrens

One spring day, I was in my tiny house in the forest, and a little bird flew through the window and started hopping on my body as I lay on my bed. I had just played with some children and felt very light and happy, just like the little bird. I felt like it was testing me to make sure I was safe. I was a big creature who wouldn't hurt a little bird.

Well, within a few days, a couple of little wrens started to make a nest inside my house. It wasn't on the eve of the porch; it was on the shelf near my computer. I allowed them to bring little bits of leaves and pine straw until their nest was complete. These birds came in and out many times per day. Some mornings, if I happened to have my windows closed, they would hop on me as if to tell me it was time to wake up and open the window.

Eventually, I heard little peeps, and the wren couple were now bringing worms and grasshoppers constantly to their nest, right above my computer work area. Friends would come over and see this in action as there was constant flying and chirping, which made it a little distracting to work. One day, as I was lying in bed in my loft, which is at the level of the shelf where the birds were nested, I woke up to little footsteps on my body. After a while, it was over. The baby birds had grown and were now outside. The parents then perched on their box and made a very loud and long singsongy conversation with me before they flew out, not to return again.

Crows and Owls

Another time, I was out in the garden and heard a lot of crows making a racket. It seemed they were upset about something and were complaining or something. I thought it was so silly, and I mimicked them just to see what would happen. I called up into the air, "Caww.... Caww....Caww." As soon as I did that, the ruckus got even louder, and it seemed angrier. Then, the twenty-five or so birds were flying around over my head! I thought I better get to my house, so I started up the hill. On my way, I called out again, "Caww....Caww...Caww," and within seconds, the sky was filled with crows. There had to have been at least two hundred. I was luckily under the cover of the forest, but they were in a frenzy and angry and flying right above the tree cover. Their sounds were deafening. I slipped into my house and shut the door.

What kind of message had I given the crows? I felt like I had broken some kind of language barrier. I was just playing around, but little did I realize I was playing with fire. For the next several days, all kinds of animals appeared for me. Everywhere I went, it seemed an eagle would be flying overhead or a deer would jump out in front of my car as it went around a blind corner.

The next night, as I was sleeping in the forest, I was awakened in the middle of the night by a loud owl. I awoke with a start, and my heart pounded as a very big owl perched above my head and continued to call out. I wouldn't dare call back to it. I crawled down inside my sleeping bag, trying to hide. What had I done? It seemed I could practically talk to any animal at will, and now they were everywhere. The owl continued for many minutes, so long that I had to just fall asleep because I couldn't stay awake any longer.

I feel these animals are not necessarily random. Native peoples around the world understand the connection between nature, animals, and the spirit realm. An animal encounter or other experience with the elements, such as weather, is considered a message being delivered or other important information that can be useful for proper action in the physical world and/or something we need to know or understand in the spiritual realm. And in order to interpret these signs, we need to look at what is going on in our lives and at our dreams and meditate on just what kind of feeling we get from an encounter. What I got from this owl was it was thanking me for saving it from the crows because crows and owls have a funny relationship, and owls are often harassed by crows where they can be singled out and pestered. Hawks also get pestered in this way, as crows gang up on them and use a mob bully mentality. This owl may have been in distress from the crows when I suddenly had the urge to call out because I felt the crows were making a lot of drama, and it was hurting my ears. The crows were offended by me, some crazy guy who was insulting them by mocking them. So they turned their anger toward me, and the owl thus escaped. Then, the owl came to thank me.

Hunting for Pine Pitch in a Pine Grove

More recently, I was out gathering pine pitch to be used in making the water-repellent fabric finish. I was wandering through a pine grove near my house, and I was feeling joy and appreciating the beauty of nature, how this magical tree can produce this healing substance that is used in medicine as well as waterproofing as well as a fire starter, a wood finish, and many other things. The sweet, sumptuous smell of the pine combined with the equally magical and healing properties of beeswax. And I was aware of how hard the bees work to make this wax. And also, there is not to this day any substitute for these gifts of nature. And the things we do to replicate something similar has resulted in the environmental disaster we see on the planet. And I felt even more inspired to introduce Lucky Sheep™ products to the world as I felt the direct connection from the earth to the sleeping bags.

The next day, I noticed a few honey bees coming into my house and buzzing around my kitchen. This normally wouldn't be a big deal; however, this was December 4, and, normally, the bees are safely hibernating in their hives this time of year. Soon, there were more, and soon, at least fifty honeybees were swarming around my tiny house. Why are they here, and what do they want? I realized they were hungry and asked me for food. I put out a plate of local honey. More came. Soon, my house was full of bees. I also put out a plate of sugar water, which they did not go to. They only wanted honey. They would not sting me. They would even land on me sometimes and tickle me. And somehow they knew to come to my house for food. Eventually, the weather turned cold again, and bees didn't come anymore. I think they were safely in their hive again.

Well, my house is a safe haven for birds as well as bees. And eagles can fly over my head any time they want. Bears now…I prefer they keep a little distance.

CHAPTER 22

My Early Initiations in Nature

How Nature Speaks — My Personal Journey

I grew up in the Wayehutta Valley in Cullowhee, North Carolina. This was a land of sparkling springs and bubbling creeks; my front and back yards were entire mountains to explore. We walked on footpaths which were called "Indian Trails;" we were told these paths were formed by the feet of the Cherokees who roamed these lands and that these lands were, in fact, the original ancestral home of the Cherokee Nation. Arrowheads were everywhere, and spring water was all I knew. My siblings and I would run barefoot in the garden, climb trees, make shelters out of sticks and leaves, and roam freely all over the vast forest, discovering new treasures with each hike. Our favorite playground toys were wild grape vines, which could be turned into swings, and seesaws made by putting logs in the crotches of trees.

All of this vanished in an instant, however, when my family moved to Kansas when I was seven. Suddenly, there were flat expanses of land with no mountains. There were sidewalks and houses seemingly on every inch of the ground. It was a shock to be taken from my childhood paradise and to realize that this would be my new reality, that this tiny town on the prairie was my new home. I kept looking for a wild place to hide and explore, but I couldn't find any. The creeks were muddy, and the water didn't even move most of the time. The rocks were jagged, dull, and ugly, unlike the polished gems found everywhere in my former mountain creeks. And the water tasted terrible. Sweet-tasting spring water was nowhere to be found.

A Realization Hits

One day in my ninth-grade history class, we were watching a documentary on the Nez Perce tribe. The Nez Perce people were the last wild tribe still roaming freely in the Northwestern US during the late 1800s. The US Calvary was sent to put an end to their lifestyle and culture by moving them to a reservation. As I sat in that darkened room, arms propped on the cold desk with the other students, I became flooded with emotions.

Thus far, in all of the history classes I had been exposed to, the white people were always portrayed as the good guys, and the Indians were the ones who were bad. Never was I shown that the white people actually stole the land and the culture from the Native Americans. But as I sat at my desk watching this film, I started to have a strange feeling. My perception of the esteemed materialistic culture around me, a culture that valued greatly having the best car and best house, clothes and everything that people pursue these days, was about to be shattered. It dawned on me as I watched these strong but peaceful and dignified people living in tipis and riding horses to hunt buffalo that these people lived in a world that seemed better than everything else surrounding me.

The film showed the conquest of these native people and their grand failed attempt at fleeing to Canada, where they had hoped that they could escape US jurisdiction. When the film ended, I was in a state of shock. What a huge loss! Living close to the earth in tipis seemed to me to be far superior to this life I found myself in, a life that was cutting me off from the outdoors and from the life force that exists everywhere in nature.

After school that day, I told my buddies that I didn't feel well and walked home alone, deep in thought. I didn't know where to start, but I knew a few things. One thing I knew was that I was not going to watch TV anymore. Watching TV made me feel sick. I had to find my own life, my own voice, my own identity. I knew that somehow, the things surrounding me and the messages coming at me were shaping me, and I wanted to know who I was, really. Because now I had nothing. Not feeling aligned or a part of my culture meant I was starting with nothing. I couldn't allow this journey of finding out who I really was to be influenced by the TV.

Another thing I knew was that I needed to write. So, I also started journaling as I sorted through my thoughts and emerging awakenings about who I was on the planet.

Questions to Contemplate:

Who are you without this current culture? Who are you without your house, your car, or your job? Who are you when immersed in and connected to nature? What happens to your identity when you don't watch TV or engage with social media for a long time? Have you practiced journaling or some other art to help you get in touch with your feelings and thoughts?

How the Indians Lived

I went to the library and found a book called *How the Indians Lived.* How did these grand, strong, dignified, and peaceful people get the way they were? How did they get the seemingly magical powers to live outdoors in the weather without modern houses and live off the land hunting wild game?

As I read the book, I saw that there were two key things. First, it was important to be outside. And one of the ways to be outside for significantly more hours a day was to sleep outside. What might happen if I slept outside instead of inside? I wanted to find out, so at fifteen years old, I started sleeping outside, dragging my sheets and blankets onto the yard in our crowded apartment complex in Lawrence, Kansas. I also got rid of the furniture in my bedroom.

Questions to Contemplate:

What might happen if you slept outside under the stars for one night? Would your sleep be different or your dreams? How about for a week? Would your sense of yourself in relation to the world change? How about a month? Would your thought patterns or emotions change? Would you feel differently about the earth, trees, and sky?

And the second key, important practice was the wearing of moccasins instead of hard-soled shoes. So I found another book, this time one on how to make moccasins, and somehow taught myself how to make them. I wore moccasins to school, along with the beaded leather headband I made.

These simple practices—sleeping outside on the earth and wearing moccasins that allow feeling and connecting to the earth through the feet—started creating a closer relationship between my body and my environment.

Outsider

People obviously thought I was crazy. Why in the world was I going backward? For example, I could easily accept a ride with a friend to school but walked all the way there instead. They didn't get it. That walking time was my therapy. I loved to walk barefoot to school, and it also gave me a sense that I wasn't stuck to someone else's agenda. I would walk many miles per day around town, to work after school, and back home. I preferred walking over riding a bicycle. At one point, I managed to not get in a car at all for two weeks, feeling cars were robbing me of a natural connection and rhythm to space and time. There was something essential that I wanted back. Somehow, I wanted to know my relationship to time, space, gravity, and body. I wanted to watch the sun travel an entire day from the beginning of sunrise to the end of sunset and feel every nuance of change that happened in between.

I didn't know who I was, but I knew that I didn't know. And I knew my teachers and peers were not helping. Instead, I could sense that there was a huge body of knowledge somewhere that would tell me. And that body of knowledge was in the silence of nature. I tried my best to get far away from human-built places, and in my little town of Lawrence, Kansas, this meant going on long bike rides and walks into the countryside. This meant even exploring my own backyard, so to speak…the places right around my house in more depth. It meant writing about my thoughts, experiences, and dreams and watching the clouds float by in the sky.

Deepening Relationships with the Spirits of Nature

I took my destiny into my own hands, and others would label me as a social misfit, a loner, and an outcast because I dropped out of organized activities and pursued my interests of walking through nature, making crafts of leather and wood, and foraging for wild plants. To me, it was a connection and entering into a wonderful world of beauty and mystery. Besides the library, where I checked out book after book about Native American history and ways, my new school was the great outdoors. I broke off from my friends in favor of my new relationship with life. I couldn't take anyone with me because they had no idea what had happened. It was as though I was suddenly struck by lightning.

And indeed, the Thunder Beings actually became my new totem power. A totem power is a Native American tradition of recognizing a personal soul kinship with certain spirits of the land, elements, plants, and animals. Lightning and thunder would be seen as a manifestation or expression of the thunder spirit or thunder beings. They also considered the eagle a Thunderbird and thus believed the eagle also had the power and qualities of the Thunder totem. I came to discover my kinship because I had several encounters with lightning as I was practically fearless of it.

One night, for example, I was camping a mile from my house on the edge of town, and the night became engulfed in a torrential thunderstorm. There was a blinding streak of lightning and thunder simultaneously so loud I could neither hear nor see for some time. What happened? Was I struck? In a few minutes, my sight came back, and the ringing in my ears stopped, and I realized I was okay. However, a tree not thirty feet from me was burning. That was a sign, a direct message from the Spirit Beings. Lightning was my power, and the Thunder Beings were my totem. This is just one example in which spending so much time understanding nature led me to understand something unique about my own makeup, my own nature.

I would often climb my favorite cottonwood tree far up into the sky, perch one foot in the crook of a limb and wrap my arms around another crook where I could write in my journal, read, or gaze into the distant prairie on one side and town on the other side. I would dream about the future and what possibilities lay beyond the horizon. Once, I went up to watch a storm coming in, blowing in from the west and was spellbound by the lightning as it got closer and closer. It had almost arrived before I finally climbed down like a cat and got back to my house, drenching wet.

Question to Contemplate:

What might you come to understand about your personal qualities by living in nature frequently? Would you find the elements, plants, rocks, water, and animals communicating with you?

My journey to find who I am really, beyond and outside of the culture I was born into, has taken me through numerous adventures, both internal and external. Much of the resulting wisdom and knowledge is in this book.

The next life-changing experience I had of self-discovery in nature in my youth was going on a Vision Quest when I was sixteen years old. Vision Quests were rites of passage for certain Native American cultures.

CHAPTER 23

My Early Vision Quest Experience

The Native American vision quest is a beautiful way of seeing how this process works. Native Peoples believe animals, plants, weather, rocks, and all of nature are alive, and we communicate back and forth. I was learning about this as I read book after book in between my boring homework assignments in high school. Books like *Black Elk Speaks* and *Rolling Thunder* made deep impressions on my young psyche.

I started having mystical experiences as if the ancestors were talking to me through the books as I read them.

Spirit Guides and Nature are one and the same thing. The world speaks to us through symbols, and each being and element in nature is a part of that language. So we don't need much to open ourselves to that world. Merely the intention and act of cultivating a relationship is all that matters. The rest follows naturally.

I went on my first self-guided vision quest the summer I was sixteen. I rcally needed to know what to do with my life. The summer I was sixteen years old, I took a Greyhound bus with my big brother to spend the summer kicking around the mountains of Western North Carolina, where I was born. That summer would change my life forever and set me on a course of adventure and creativity that would never stop, even to this day.

I was trying to figure out just how this works and wondering if I would hear a voice in a tree or see something magical happen. I had no shaman to guide me, so I just kept stumbling along, trying to figure it out. Little did I know that the whole time I was looking for something to just fall out of the sky, I was perfectly held and protected by my own spirit guides who, later, someday, I would wake up to.

One day in early June, I packed a daypack with only a few things like a rain poncho, rock hammer, and tree field guide and headed up the mountain behind my boyhood home in Cullowhee, North Carolina. This was the ancestral lands of the Cherokee Nation, a.k.a. Nantahala National Forest. I was walking in the area near a sacred site called Judaculla Rock. This rock has petroglyphs depicting the story of a giant who once ruled the area and is found in the tales of the Cherokee to this day. For the next four days, I walked and listened in silence with no food and prayed for a vision. I journaled as I observed everything happening. A cloud would blow by as I was walking. *Was that a sign? Perhaps it was taking on a special animal shape?* An owl would call out in the night. *Was that a sign? What is it telling me?* This whole time, nothing significant seemed to happen. Maybe this was all nonsense, after all? Who was I to try to interpret these things I'd only read about in books? When was I going to get my vision? What was my life going to be about? I found trails along the ridge and kept walking until I walked off the edge of the map I carried, somewhere near the Blue Ridge Parkway, near Balsam. After four days of wandering, hungry, thirsty, and bedraggled, I followed logging roads, which finally brought me to a highway. I walked up to a stranger's house to call my dad, got kicked away by the first one and searched for another neighbor who was more friendly. My dad showed up shortly after.

I was trying to figure out what my vision was. What was my totem, my guidance? Was it the owl that came nearby one night? Was it the rain that almost came but didn't quite? Or was it one of my dreams, or all of them put together? There was nothing vivid and clear. However, I would never look at life the same. I had walked four days and three nights with practically nothing through the mountains and forest, I slept with no tent over my head, and I felt like there was no longer fear about going into the woods, going to the edge of my comfort zone, or exploring the world.

Later that summer, when all the adventures were finished, the Greyhound bus brought my brother and me back to our home on the great plains of Lawrence, Kansas. That fearlessness I had experienced from the vision quest carried over into my new life as I entered my first year in high school. I was now adapted to the wild, and I knew where I came from. That gave me the strength to face the crazy challenges and opportunities that the new year would open up. I took a big leap in owning my destiny and calling the shots instead of other people and "the system" doing it for me. Many years later, this would be known as "badassery," especially considering I had no role models besides my far-off and long-lost big brother, who had suggested the Vision Quest and described how to do it in a letter that I had carried with me. For the most part, I was coming up with this through my own connection with nature and spirit.

PART 7

Nature Poetry

Wind and rain and chirping songs
that go on all day long
How could anything here be wrong?

The light of the sun and waters that run
Make gold between the shadows of the dancing green ones
where life seems so fresh and undone.

Sleepy-eyed in the time of the dawn
where thoughts are so fresh and long
like the awakening of an unborn fawn

The roar of the bear and the crashing falls
demands a dare of your physical all
when on the mountains so tall.

From the peaks you can see
the lakes and the trees
so great you feel like a tiny bee.

so graceful are the hawks
swaying and looping as if to mock
the slowness of our walk.

and the harmony in the air
that the water wind and birds share
is such that no symphony can compare.

The water sings of the life if brings
to the plants and all living things
which make the cycle ring
for the existence of our very being.

(Poem Written on my Vision Quest, June 4, 1980)

Fairy Dust

All night long the fairies blew their breath
Into the air

and now
It pours over the valley

Like a whisper surrounding the trees
the rocks the plants

We wake up slowly from dreams
half remembered

Softly yawning
All sound is gone

Absorbed by the mist
What did we learn?

Thoughts and sounds dissolved
Into fine particles

White, wispy
All earth soil plants smell
Mixed into sweet moist ambrosia
Be still
There is no need to move

Absorb the freshest of the fresh
Into your pores
The Forest's gift
Breath deep
Remember

Full moon beaming light,
water crashing singing all night,
surrounded by rocks and bubbles moving continuously
Renewing
there is no past or future where I slept
and I am infused with complete sparkly possibilities
unknown and unmanifest
yet fresh and waking up
to an icy dip
where my bedroom and home
is the entire universe

Take Only What You Can Carry

It twirls and swirls
It whirls and whines
It twirls and swirls
It dies down but suddenly picks up
All the trees are shaking
Sun goes over one side of the mountain and the day
The full moon pours from the other side
I feel everything, the cold icing its way
Through my clothing
The air piercing my nostrils with its bite
I get my tent pitched in the nick of time
A little food cooked in the dark
And sit spooning soup and melted butter into my mouth
I am warm. I am safe.
I walk around camp feeling everything.
I howl at the moon
The wind howls back like a pack of wolves
The wind and ice
My tent and bed ready for evening
Staked tightly to the ground
It twirls and swirls
It lifts and rifts
It whirls and whines
The moonlight pours
Onto the mountain
Through the trees
Yelling and swinging
Playing and swaying
Ferocious, just the sound alone
Would turn most people away

Through my canvas tent
I cover my eyes.
And listen and feel
I feel the inside and the outside
I feel a stillness no one could see
It is what I will take with me
When I die

Only what I can pack into my backpack
And carry on my back
—not even—
It is what protects me from the winds of life
And right now makes me feel full
Even though, this is all I have
Shields me from imbalanced emotions and wrong thinking
Both the guilt and the blame
From judging and the need to judge
It is the stillness and the emptiness
Having just enough
Because too much won't fit in the pack
And too little, you wouldn't survive.

My Bones Remember

My bones know these waters—
Big Creek, upstream, the place near where I grew up.

They tumble and bubble,
Foam and smash,
Crash and bounce,
Sing and dance.

Ricochet down the mountain,
Over boulders, logs, moss,
Playing with the fish and salamanders
On their way, passing through
The valley they carved.

They sparkle and shine
In rays of mist,
Mixed with dappled sunlight.

My bones know this well.
My bones remember—
And sink down into
A peace,
A silence with no
Coming nor going,
Yet nothing but
Coming and going.

A stillness hanging in between
Each coming and going,
In a timeless time,
A placeless place,
Between worlds.

I slept by the water all night long
And woke up feeling a pain long buried.
My bones remembered
Because they knew these waters
From the beginning.

I sit on this boulder,
Water swirling on all sides,
Breathing in a smell so sweet,
I cannot leave.

I can feel the pain lingering from the past.

I come from a story
I did not want to remember—
A pain that, to relive,
Would destroy.

But here, it's okay.

Here, by this stream,
It will pass through me.

I tried to forget,
But these waters persisted.
Would not stop singing—

This happened.
This was your life.
But this was not you.

See this.
Acknowledge this.
Feel this.
And then,
Let it pass.

These waters heal.

These waters sing the song of the stars,
Twinkling in the night sky—
Wide, cold, pure, deep—
Constant, cutting through millennia
To get to the core,
Right where the truth is.
These waters sing
The story of the universe.

You can hear it—
If you can stand to listen.
If it doesn't kill you first.

Most cannot bear to hear.
Could not bear to listen and feel.

Sit and sleep beside the creek—
And you will be pure.
You will become the sound,
The music, the energy.

Nothing will be left inside you.
It gets washed away,
One grain at a time,
Until you become silent.

You become truth.
And you exist—
Whole and complete.

Between worlds.
Between time and space.

Often, you will want to turn and run.
Go find something to do.
Find some people to
Validate you, entertain you.
Anything to get away.

But sit here.
Sleep here.
Walk here.
Be here.

Breathe the mist deep into your center core.
Hear the pounding of the river—
On the bank,
And further away.

Feel its power
And how it changes you.
Move with it.
Stay with it.

Your story—
Of who you are, where you came from—
Goes downstream,
Or evaporates.

Now, you are ever new—
Fresh, vibrant, unencumbered.

You are—
Boulders.
Mist.
Ancient Trees.
Water.
Silence.

And your bones remember.

www.ingramcontent.com/pod-product-compliance
Lightning Source LLC
Chambersburg PA
CBHW070100030426
42335CB00016B/1953